# The Small Town Church

*Creative Leadership Series*

# The Small Town Church

## Peter J. Surrey

*Creative Leadership Series*
*Lyle E. Schaller, Editor*

Abingdon / Nashville

# THE SMALL TOWN CHURCH

## Library of Congress Cataloging in Publication Data

SURREY, PETER J (PETER JOHN), 1928-
   The small town church.
   (Creative leadership series)
   1. Small churches. 2. Rural churches. I. Title. II. Series.
   BV637.8.S93        254'.24        81-622
                                AACR2

### ISBN 0-687-38720-5

The author and publisher acknowledge with thanks—

The Christian Century Foundation for permission to reproduce in a slightly different form "Changes in a Small Church? Never!" and "The Patients Are So Hopeful," which appeared originally in *The Christian Century* and *The Christian Ministry* respectively. Copyrighted by The Christian Century Foundation, 1979. All rights reserved.

Harper & Row for permission to reproduce as an epigraph for chapter 2, an excerpt from *Brave New World* by Aldous Huxley. Copyrighted 1932, 1960 by Aldous Huxley. Reprinted by permission of Harper & Row, Publishers, Inc.

Viking Penguin, Inc., for permission to reproduce as an epigraph for chapter 9, an extract from *Travels with Charley* by John Steinbeck. Copyrighted © 1961, 1962 by the Curtis Publishing Company. Copyrighted © 1962 by John Steinbeck. Reprinted by permission of Viking Penguin, Inc.

Violet Alleyn Storey for permission to reproduce as an epigraph for chapter 3, an extract from her poem "Ironical," copyrighted by Miss Storey.

Scripture quotations are the author's translation or from the King James Version of the Bible.

MANUFACTURED BY THE PARTHENON PRESS AT
NASHVILLE, TENNESSEE, UNITED STATES OF AMERICA

To Doctor Hussey and Howard
laymen who work in the small church

# Foreword

"This is a small parish in a small town. Probably neither the parish nor the town can be expected to change much."

In only twenty-two words the seventy-year-old Mary Walsh offers some very wise advice to the recently arrived young minister who had been hoping to find himself in a new suburban parish.

The small town is a distinctive social organization in North America. It is not a small scale model of the city! The city is built on a foundation of specialized functions. The small town owes its unique character to a complex web of interpersonal relationships. That is one reason why the residents of the typical small town frequently oppose growth, why they see the city as an interesting place to visit but not as an attractive place to live, and why it is so difficult for newcomers to gain a sense of belonging in a small town. That network of relationships sustains people, offers meaning to life, and tends to exclude newcomers until they are awarded a place in that web of relationships.

That emphasis on interpersonal relationships also explains why roots, ancestry, "good bloodlines," and continuity are such important dimensions of life in the small town. It is easier and quicker to "earn a place" in an urbanized society based on the specialized functions of civilization than to gain a sense of belonging in a culture built on relationships. Recruits in the peacetime army, the mother-in-law who moves in with her son and daughter-in-law, and the new member of the small-town church—all discover this as they reflect on their feelings of being "left out" of that network of relationships.

In this series of letters to the minister of a small-town parish Peter J. Surrey describes the culture of the small town and explains how this context shapes the values, life, goals, expectations, and standards of the small-town church.

While the book is filled with humorous situations and insights, this is a very serious volume. It not only can be of great help to the minister going out to serve a small-town congregation, it also can be of tremendous value to the leaders of the small-town church as they see various facets of their own parish reflected in what goes on at St. Stephen's. After reading this series of letters, these leaders will be able to look at their own congregations and see more clearly what is happening, why it is happening that way, and why what may appear to some to be trivial details are really important events. Frequently these trivial items of gossip represent major changes in that mosaic of relationships and that is why they are important. Mary Walsh knows that, and the alert reader will benefit from her wisdom.

This also is an affirming book. The author affirms the value of relationships, roots, symbolism, continuity, and stability. These are basic concepts in understanding both the small-town society and the small-town parish. The creative leader will see the value of these concepts and use them as foundation stones in planning for the future of the church in the small town.

Lyle E. Schaller
Yokefellow Institute
Richmond, Indiana

# Contents

# Preface

Some sixty miles from the southern end of Lake Huron, there lies a beautiful cove which is beyond the power of a painter to paint and outside the strength of a poet to describe. On fair days the clear water reflects the warmth of the sun; on calm nights the pine trees shadow this bay until the rising moon dispels the darkness.

Beyond the beach are people living in a town called Bypass. To the occasional traveler, Bypass seems sleepy and quiet, but there is always human drama present in this small town of five thousand. Now the conflicts, desires, and hopes that contribute to this drama create lessons to be learned, and nowhere in town can this better be done than among the two hundred souls who make up the parish known as Saint Stephen's.

Of course, Saint Stephen's and Bypass spring from my imagination, but the lessons they illustrate were learned in such places as Little Current, Ontario, Lynn Lake, Manitoba, Watseka, Illinois, and Savanna, Illinois. In a real way Trinity College, Toronto, and the University of Illinois also contributed to this book.

I am grateful to all of them.

May all those who read this work, pastors and laymen alike, be aided while ". . . . attending to the duties of the Sanctuary."

# I

# Want an Attractive Parish, Pastor?
# Try Bypass!

"By the way, Mr. Watson, would you like a tropical climate? The Marquesas, for example; or Samoa? Or something rather more bracing?"

Helmholtz rose from his pneumatic chair. "I should like a thoroughly bad climate," he answered. "I believe one would write better if the climate were bad. If there were a lot of wind and storms, for example." (Aldous Huxley—*Brave New World*)

The Cathedral
Diocesan City

Dear Paul,

My mind is made up, and I am afraid that you are not going to like the decision. Which is another way of telling you that you will not be assigned to Grace Church, Country Club Hills. Instead, you will be going to Saint Stephen's mission, Bypass, Michigan. Of course you can refuse to go and Saint Stephen's can refuse to take you; but since I am the bishop I do not expect either event to happen. That is as good as saying that it will not! Believe me, I did not make this choice lightly. To put it another way, I have two excellent reasons for my action, and this letter is being written to explain them. The first concerns Saint Stephen's itself; the second concerns you. I am going to take each in turn.

Saint Stephen's is an old high church country parish with no more than fifty families. Perhaps you might be forced to count a few dogs and cats to come up with even that number! It has been around for more than 125 years—and looks it. All its property is old and in desperate need of repair. The last pastor reported that this was also true of some of its people—especially a woman parishioner by the name of Joy Jones. Mrs. Jones and he had several battles. According to both Mr. Arthur J. Fillmore and Miss Mary Walsh, most of the trouble seems to have arisen because Joy is very outspoken and the rector was just too sensitive. Dean Upchurch concluded that we just had the wrong man in the wrong place and that the clergyman involved would be better in a suburban location. Therefore, after a good deal of soul-searching, I have nominated him for Country Club Hills in the hope that this will become his niche. At any rate . . . try to get along with Mrs. Jones, for she is related to some of the old and leading town families. And that brings me to an important point.

In your application for Country Club Hills, you stated that you liked the newness of the congregation. This is in direct contrast to Saint Stephen's, Bypass. Not only is Grace Church, Country Club Hills new; it is also very fluid. Had you gone there you would have been lucky to find half the members of your January vestry still with you in December. Change will be the rule at Grace Church, while the appearance of a new woman in the kitchen hierarchy at Saint Stephen's will call for comment.

Again, Country Club Hills gives the appearance of being in the center of modern American life, while Bypass impresses strangers as geographically and ideologically isolated. Actually, this impression needs to be modified. From a historical and practical point of view Bypass is closer to what the average American thinks American communities ought to be, and it is Country Club Hills which seems less than ideal. Americans, despite their habit of roaming, do not like places that have no roots. Country Club Hills has almost none, while Bypass, if anything, has far too many. Yet change is coming to most American small towns and also to churches they contain. I am afraid that Saint Stephen's is not very partial to transformations. In their own high-church fashion, these new parishioners of yours have their own traditions and you will be expected to fit into them. Please do!

Despite all this, why do I feel that you can do more good at Saint Stephen's than at Grace? The reason springs from what your former principal, Theophilus K. Ignatius, told me about you. Our parish in Bypass has a poor image of itself. It needs a person who is buoyant and full of zest. When the time comes to end your ministry at Saint Stephen's, I have great hopes that the people will be the richer for it. Your work will not be easy, for boosting morale is never easy. Perhaps a few suggestions would be acceptable?

Criticism of the congregation must be avoided at all costs. You will have to cultivate patience. Praise everything that is done well. I would not be the bishop if I did not say, "Encourage your parishioners to take part in as many diocesan activities as possible." And please have those buildings fixed in order that the people can take pride in their property and not be forced to apologize to the rest of the community for their appearance.

Obviously, your attitude toward all this will be crucial. I know that you are eager to advance in your profession. That is not necessarily a bad thing, providing that you use and turn your ambition toward Saint Stephen's. Of course, pride and ambition can become very great sins if they are used for personal glory. Still . . . if one stops and thinks about it . . . Jesus, in his parable of the talents praised ambition, and it can certainly be argued that Saint Paul took great pride in the work he did.

At this stage in the letter, let me read your mind. "Ha,"

15

you are saying to yourself, "would it not be possible to use my talents at Country Club Hills? Do they not need a church building in that area? Will it not be necessary to recruit people? Could not I use my training in order to organize this new parish?" These are good questions! But what are they really saying? Is it not that the demands at Country Club Hills are greater than the demands at Bypass?

Bluntly, the answer is no. The necessity at Bypass is greater because on the surface there seems to be no necessity. In a real way you will have to dig in order to discover the challenge and, having discovered it, you will have to let the congregation also learn about it. The idea is certainly worth exploring further.

Once a parish becomes established—when its buildings have been erected and paid for and its programs created—it has a tendency to lose enthusiasm. Christian life must have structure; but it must also be recognized that structure, once established, has a habit of choking off life. Indeed, I have a friend who feels that as a matter of policy all church organizations should be smashed once a generation and that everybody should then start all over again with nothing but raw Christian faith. This notion is as old as the piece of biblical wisdom that points out that men do not put new wine into old wineskins for fear that the old wineskins will break. On the other hand, small churches do not take kindly to pastors who try to destroy their structure. Thus, for better or for worse, you will have to find ways of doing things in a fashion that the Bible says is not wise. Old wineskins are going to have to stand up to new ideas, and you will have the thankless task of making the old wineskins like it! You cannot hope to change deep-seated traditions; you can only hope to harness them.

Your major asset, which Dr. Theophilus K. Ignatius spotted, must be brought into action. It is your imagination! At the present time Country Club Hills does not need a great dose of imagination; what it has to have is a pastor with

16

much tact, persuasive power, and the ability to choose from the good lay leadership that lies at hand. Opposite to this is the fact that you will not have many good lay leaders because you do not have many people. Somehow you will be forced to utilize those you do have to the utmost, and somehow you will have to try and induce those who have no inclination for pacesetting to become more active in the parish. This is why I place so much importance on that priceless commodity known as imagination.

Unfortunately, the use of that skill comes with a price—the price of frequent failure. Often your congregation will reject your ideas. Many rectors in large parishes are careful to screen their contacts with people through the use of secretaries, appointment books, and a busy schedule. You, Paul, will enjoy no such chance for rationalizations; for, to a large extent, you will have to make your own opportunities. Perhaps the chief way the Holy Spirit can work at Saint Stephen's is through you. In the beginning at least, your satisfactions will have to come from your ministry at the local level.

What can these satisfactions be? One will lie in the fact that you will become the master of many trades—maintenance man, pastor, public relations expert, preacher, financial wizard, rural sociologist, operator of office machines, builder, teacher, and priest. After your ministry at Saint Stephen's is over, you will be equipped to deal with many more situations than you are at present.

Internally, you will have to learn how to cope with many negative emotions—especially the one known as fear—and how to use that coping power to your advantage. Externally, self-discipline will have to take hold of your conscience, and real Christian love must penetrate your soul. In short, you will grow in a Christian sense, or you will perish.

It might be interesting for you to keep a diary. From it you could write to me from time to time and inform me of your

17

progress, measuring it against those criteria I have outlined. Have a happy and successful ministry at Bypass, Paul.

With all good wishes,
T. Cranmer, Bishop

# II

# That Town, Bypass!
# Ogre or Cherub?

I have a small town soul.
It makes me want to know
Wee, unimportant things
About the folks that go . . . (Violet Alleyn Storey)

Canterbury Street
Palestine, Michigan

**Highly Confidential**

Dear Paul,

How the following information fell into my hands is interesting, but of limited importance. Sufficient to say that it concerns the town of Bypass, Michigan—where shortly you will be stationed. All of it was left in my keeping in order that I might make a critical examination of its contents. In exchange for my appraisal, the author had given me permission to use his notes for my religious column—providing I use the utmost discretion. Therefore, although he is allowing me to release some of this information to you, it is with the understanding that you will allow nobody else to view it. Since the author—a Reverend Nominis Expers, a pastor of the Christian Church of Upper Scurra—has used the actual names of people and places, this caution must be doubly emphasized.

In other words . . . until you send this manuscript back to me, or to the bishop . . . keep it under lock and key!

With all good wishes,
A. M. Upchurch, Dean

# THE CULTURE OF BYPASS MICHIGAN—
## A STUDY IN PARADOX
### BY
## THE REVEREND NOMINIS EXPERS
### AS
## PART OF THE REQUIREMENTS
## FOR A MASTER'S DEGREE
### IN
## THE DEPARTMENT OF FOREIGN CULTURAL STUDIES
### OF
## UPPER SCURRA UNIVERSITY

### Society

The society of Bypass, Michigan, can best be described as highly stratified, individualistic, work-oriented . . . and hidden. To a large extent the natives understand the main traditions and forces that hold their town together, but it is open to question as to how well the residents know the more subtle workings of this community. This fact was brought out when people chosen at random were asked to place themselves and certain specific neighbors in different social strata. Nobody called himself or herself upper class, even when their neighbors did so. Everybody with one exception identified Arthur J. Fillmore, the town banker, as the most influential man in town. That one exception, of course, was Arthur J. Fillmore.

The dominant culture of the community is white, of

northern European extraction, and Protestant in religion. The area is supported by many orchards. At harvest migrants, mostly of Mexican and Spanish extraction, are imported into the area. Although the town welcomes their labor and encourages them to spend money locally, none stay after the harvest is over. Some five miles away there is a small Indian reservation, and a few of these Native Americans have drifted into Bypass as permanent residents. Their effect is minimal.

## Open or Closed Society?

The first impression a stranger receives of this small town is the way it works at being friendly. On my first morning, while I was on my way to the "Broiler of Bypass" for breakfast, at least three complete strangers greeted me. Once it was understood, however, that I was making a sociological study of the town, many of the inhabitants became hesitant about answering my questions. I have since learned that this is a common attitude among members of small American communities.

Several individuals who had lived in Bypass for less than five years confirmed this fact by stating that this same caution and suspicion extended to them. As they put it, "This town has never accepted us." It is obvious that Bypass makes newcomers earn their standing in the town.

Until late this morning I was going to leave this section of my manuscript at that point . . . but then I conversed with the mayor of Bypass. His feelings are worth recording, although it was obvious from the very beginning that he was more interested in teasing me than in adding to my knowledge about his town. As near as memory permits, I shall quote him verbatim and without further comment.

"Well, Reverend, we have exercised Christian charity and hired Glen Walsh as the new town clerk."

"The man who was convicted of embezzling money at Harvey Lightfoot's trucking concern?"

21

"The same."

"Won't you have a reaction from the citizens?"

"I don't think so. Glen comes from an old and respected Bypass family. He has lived here a long time. Everybody knows him. And after all . . . we didn't make him the town treasurer!"

## Determining Individual Social Status

The easiest way to have social standing in Bypass is to be born into a family with an upper-class position. The next best thing is to be related to a family that enjoys such a rank. If you are a stranger, come with a profession that the community recognizes as important. Doctors and bankers fill that category quite well; lawyers and people who own their own business, only a little less well. Teachers and clergy will have to wait longer before the community knows and values them. Wealth, or at least the appearance of wealth, is a great aid in winning acceptance providing the person does not flaunt it; people in small towns have a tendency to suspect an individual who tries to impress them by great ostentation of any sort.

At the lowest end of the scale will be those who move to Bypass without economic resources or family connections. Since many people in this category sought help from the church at which I was temporarily stationed as pastor, I took the opportunity to question several. Often I discovered serious money difficulties and searing emotional plights. Quite literally, the sins of the fathers have a bad habit of being visited upon the children; for many times people are born into a situation that demands steadiness of purpose and a deep, stable control of feelings. Frequently, these elements seem to be lacking. In Bypass many citizens see those who belong to this category as the authors of their misfortunes—a judgment that seems too harsh. As the chief of police once observed to the local ministerial association:

"These are men and women who do not fit into our society. Many have severe alcohol problems; others have to labor under severe family difficulties. As much as one might wish to help, it must be understood that many do not want the aid they need. In any case, Bypass is not well equipped to give it."

In between these strata fall the greatest number of the community's citizens. Most of them like to be as independent as possible in as many ways as possible. I was surprised to discover the number of natives who considered themselves happy. Continually, they informed me that they like to visit the city, but they would never want to live there; the companionship, interest, and love of their friends would be missed too much.

## Volunteer and Lesser Government Organizations

It follows that residents of this area like individuals they know to work for them in positions of public responsibility. Newcomers must wait before they will be elected as officers in community and club organizations. Indeed "election" is not the correct term; people are appointed and then elected. The machinery for doing this is called "a nominating committee"—a most fascinating method for circumventing democracy. The nominating committee is always appointed by the chairman or president of the organization. This little appointed group carefully observes several rules. For example, they know that no person on such a committee can nominate himself for a position. They also understand clearly that no great changes in policies are wanted. Individuals selected by this nominating committee will always meet the standards of conservatism and social standing that the other members feel are appropriate. People put forward by the nominating committtee are almost always assured of election.

Lesser elected government bodies in Bypass—this includes

23

such groups as the Cemetery Board and the Park District—turn their entire membership into a nominating committee and will make certain that all vacancies are filled before election time. Incumbents almost always run for reelection, and the local Bypass natives understand that they are to be returned to office. Consequently, should some brave soul have himself placed on the ballot without a suitable invitation from the board to which he is seeking membership, he can expect to be defeated. Bypass citizens seem to like their boards to be self-perpetuating.

As an additional note, it is worth pointing out that calling these organizations "lesser elected bodies" is a bit of a misnomer, for frequently they control property worth many hundreds of thousands of dollars.

## Main Government Bodies

The main government of Bypass is looked after by six councilmen and their head, who is called the mayor. Their task is to make budgets, run such services as street and alley maintenance, and see that refuse is collected and that the right laws are passed which are necessary for the well-being of all the citizens. The other major government body in town is the school board. This august group employs over one hundred people, has a budget that is almost as large as the one enjoyed by the mayor and council, and is elected every four years by Bypass citizens. One would assume that these two groups, having won their positions after long campaigns, should give equal weight to the opinions of each citizen—but everybody in town assured me that this was not the case. Constantly, as I interviewed residents on their government, I heard about a group called the Family Compact, whose influence was considered to be substantial in the affairs of the town.

For my own elucidation, I chose twenty residents of Bypass at random and then asked them to compile for me the names of those who belonged to this governing group. If the people were not named by at least 80 percent of my volunteers, I did not include them in the list outlined below. As the reader peruses the list, he is asked to note that, with one exception, none of the six names belonged either to the school board or to the town council—indeed four of them seem to shun public office altogether.

## The Bypass Family Compact

| Name | Occupation | Reasons Given for Belonging to Family Compact |
|------|-----------|-----------------------------------------------|
| Arthur J. Fillmore | President, Bypass State Bank. | Old family of Bypass. Wealthy. |
| Michael "Poke" Smith | Mortician. On board of Bypass State Bank. | Owns large business. Third-generation Bypass family. Good friend of Arthur J. Fillmore. On town council. |
| James Charles Walsh | Executive Director, Bypass Building and Loan. President, Bypass Fruit Cooperative. Member, Michigan Legislature. | Brother-in-law of Arthur J. Fillmore. Old Bypass family. Wife also from old Bypass family. Wealthy. |
| Mrs. Herbert P. Jackson (widow) | Large real estate owner. Fortune inherited from activities of grandfather-in-law during Prohibition. | Mrs. Jackson, although of Spanish-Mexican descent, married into a wealthy Bypass family. Rumored to have influence over Arthur J. Fillmore. Admired by women of Family Compact. |

25

| Name | Occupation | Reasons Given for Belonging to Family Compact |
|------|------------|-----------------------------------------------|
| Dr. Henry C. Jones | Dentist, on board of Bypass State Bank and Fruit Cooperative. Owns several fruit farms. | Lived in Bypass for many years. Has elite dental practice. Wife, Joy, is cousin of Arthur J. Fillmore's wife. |
| Philip G. Jones | Owner of large automobile agency and several fruit farms. On board of Bypass Building and Loan. | Friend of Arthur J. Fillmore. Brought to town by dentist brother to take over then bankrupt automobile agency. Now rumored to be quite wealthy. |

The methods of control exercised by the Family Compact seem quite indirect. The power of the clique is not absolute; none of the members would be foolish enough to challenge elected officials directly. Hints, carefully dropped suggestions at business and social gatherings, and, if necessary, a brief comment by its town council member are sufficient to let everybody know how the Family Compact feels on matters. Indeed, the group relies on restraint, preferring that the community members understand its general policies more than specific suggestions.

## Opposition to the Family Compact

Within the town of Bypass there is a group of professional and business people anxious to take over the role of the Family Compact should its influence ever decline. This gathering centers around the "Fruitlands Building and Loan." The leading power in this association is one Harvey James Lightfoot, the owner of a trucking firm, who moved into the area about twenty years ago from another community called Cranberry Portage. Harvey has been successful in financing several of his friends through the Cranberry Portage National Bank, but his attempts to bring other businesses into the area that would rival those owned by members of the Family Compact have largely failed. The latest, a funeral home, had three burials in as many years and is now out of business. From these attempts and failures I assume that the residents of Bypass either like the way the Family Compact does things or, in their turn, are reluctant to challenge its established positions.

### Divorced Families

In Upper Scurra, if there is sufficient cause, one is allowed to divorce one's children, one's parents, or one's spouse. In Bypass, divorce is limited to getting rid of one's husband or wife. This restraint leads to all sorts of difficulties. Generally, the wife is given the children, but when she remarries—this is very common—the children do not assume their new father's name except in special circumstances. Consequently, the visitor from Upper Scurra may discover many people living under one roof who have several last names among them. This is confusing, so I have included a number of social rules to cover this problem.

1. Never ask anybody living in the household to explain the circumstances. In Bypass this is impolite. Observe and determine as much as you can yourselves.

2. Always show by your words and actions that you accept the situation—however strange it may seem by Upper Scurra standards.

3. In Bypass, it is the task of a friend or relative of the family to explain the circumstances of the marriage. When you are accepted in the community, they will tell you what they feel you should know.

4. If you are extremely puzzled by the circumstances, it is

27

permissible to ask a friend or a neighbor about the relationships of the family in question; but one should always couch such demands in a discreet fashion.

## Use of Titles

In Upper Scurra, when addressing a person, it is polite to put his or her title before the individual's last name. Among the residents of Bypass, it is customary always to use the first name of people—with the exception of clerics, judges, and doctors—whenever possible. This rule is especially important in introductions. Thus one says, "Meet Art Fillmore!" and not, "May I introduce you to Mr. Fillmore, the president of the Bypass State Bank?"

## Some Common Bypass Expressions

1. *How are you?* This is merely a polite greeting. The speaker is not interested in the state of your health. Even if you are dying you are expected to say, "Very well, thank you."

2. *Pastor:* In Upper Scurra a cleric can be a *pastor* who holds a *pastorate* in a *pastoral* setting. In Bypass the word has become a verb—as in the sentence "I have pastored this church for five years."

3. *Coffee Klatch:* Almost no social event in Bypass is complete without coffee. Your more informal meetings are called "coffee klatches." (The spelling of the latter word varies from person to person.) Newcomers should observe these informal gatherings carefully, for they will disclose social patterns, the transaction of business deals, and the manner in which much information is transmitted. Not to offer a visitor coffee is frequently a sign that you wish him or her to leave.

4. *Dinner:* In Upper Scurra this always refers to the noon meal; in Bypass it refers to the amount of food to be served

by your hostess. A polite visitor to Bypass from Upper Scurra should always make sure of the hour; for a dinner can be served at many different times, depending on the family and the occasion being celebrated.

## Conclusion

It is a solemn matter to analyze a community of another nation; the author must warn the reader that his study is far from exhaustive. Nevertheless, he hopes that it will aid the inhabitants of Upper Scurra to appreciate the complex workings of that most interesting social grouping—the American small town.

# III

# Changes in the Small Church? Never!

Be we High or Low, the Status is Quo. (Old Episcopal Saying)

10 Church Street
Bypass, Michigan

Dear Pastor,

It was only after much hesitation that I decided to write you this letter. Last week's meeting between you and the Women's Guild does call for a few observations! In the course of my seventy years, I have seen many clashes between parishioners and clergy and they do upset me. For as long as I can remember, I have loved this little parish and the clergy who have served it as pastors; and it has always seemed to me that many difficulties between them could have been avoided if both sides could have recognized the basic values of the other. Many times lay people expect clergy to respond to subtle cues and chance remarks, while clergy, seeking to maintain their ministerial image, fail to express their true feelings. Consequently, both parties frequently become involved in what the lawyers call an adversary position. Too often the victim in all of this is the parish. To illustrate what I mean, let us go back to the guild meeting of last week.

You began by remarking on our low Sunday attendance. Then you reviewed the bills and the budget. The main explosion was provoked by your innocent comment—or was it so innocent?—on the old furnishings of the sanctuary. "All that old stuff," you said, "is so dreadful that it looks as though it had been handmade by the monkeys in Noah's ark!" As a matter of interest, you were closer to the truth than you realized.

The women's reactions were even more revealing. Joy Jones spent loving moments on the state of the washrooms and simply refused to listen to our problems about obtaining a janitor. Josephine's observations about your not joining Rotary did appear a little off the subject; but, given her set of values, they were not surprising. You did not like it when the conversation turned to Jim Clancy's matrimonial adventures. Anne had come to that meeting armed with this information, and she simply had to tell it before too many of the women left!

I suppose that if we are ever going to explain ourselves to each other, we had better state some basic facts. First of all, this is a small parish in a small town. Probably neither the parish nor the town can be expected to change much. That fact is the clue for understanding the entire situation. Small churches are not smaller editions of large churches, any more than my Volkswagen Beetle is a small Cadillac. Historically, small churches are on the fringe of denominational attention and thus are less influenced by central decisions than are larger parishes.

People, however, cannot live in a vacuum; and so we have built up our traditions, some of which have nothing to do with the policies or influences of the larger church. Unfortunately, this means that we have a certain way of looking at things, and this "way" is often hidden and difficult to grasp. Often lay people will go to great lengths to make sure the pastor does not understand them. Many of your people's ideas are quite opposite to yours and to the hopes of the national church.

In a sense—and I know this may be difficult to grasp—you,

31

as the pastor, are a threat to a small church. This sort of thing goes back at least to Saint Paul, who, I understand, had a difficult time with his parishes in Corinth and Galatia. The chief problem with Saint Paul was that he wanted his entire parish to go straight to heaven at the precise moment he converted them, while his parishioners kept saying, "We'll be glad to go, Paul, but we have a few other interests we would like to deal with first." All of us in Bypass are interested in salvation, but all of us have interests in the church that frequently lie outside the church's chief purpose. May I be a bit presumptuous and begin with you?

As I see you (and most clergy), you are always looking forward to the future. Pastors want more and more worshipers on Sunday and more and more programs during the week. It is always a source of satisfaction when a pastor can report more baptisms and more children and teachers in the church school than in previous years. Growth means that more bills can be paid. Advancement in your profession is often measured in terms of a larger membership, whether you had anything to do with the growth or not. The system forces you to be forward looking.

Second, clergy live with statistics, but statistics tend to make parishioners abstract. There is no way of reporting to headquarters that Mrs. Jones came back to church after a year's absence because she was worried about her sick son, or that Bob Thomas suddenly upped his pledge because he was thankful for the success of his surgery. Your parishioners, in other words, are human and have human responses; but there is no way of getting such facts on a computer printout.

Third, clergy have a tendency to seek their satisfactions outside the small church. They look outward, toward headquarters or toward meetings or toward books for their inspirations and new ideas. It is hard for parishioners to appreciate this attitude, despite the fact that they may be well educated themselves. People in small towns value pastors in terms of their ability to be known and liked. A sense of humor, an ability to read social cues, a willingness to become "one of the boys or girls" (provided you know where to stop)—these are what small communities value in their pastors. If questioned on such matters most search committees would deny that these are the qualities they want in a pastor. But do not let such denials fool you!

Against these points of view are the traditions your church people believe in. I think of them in terms of three loves—first, love of the past; then, love of order; and, finally, love toward each other. We will take each of these in turn.

Opposite to your tendency to look to the future, a small congregation is much more likely to look toward the past. A recent visitor from headquarters called us "backward looking"; and, although this opinion needs to be modified, there is much truth in the remark. The need for modification lies in the fact that, if our values are to survive, we must pass them on to future generations. We do this all the time. When Mrs. Slatterly warned the younger girls last Easter to be careful with the altar cross because it was a memorial to Jim Hope, who had been killed in World War II, she was educating them about their heritage. It is your task to teach newcomers about Christian behavior and that sort of thing; it is our task to make sure that newcomers know about local traditions. You might sum us up by making a comparison with Henry Ford, for it was he, I believe, who said that "history is more or less bunk." If by some great stretch of the imagination Henry had become our pastor, he would not have lasted a week!

All this is leading up to your attempt to replace that sanctuary furniture. In case you did not know it, that set was given many years ago by the family who founded the church. Oh, we all know their bodies are out in the cemetery; but, as long as we have that altar and all that goes with it, these people in a very spiritual sense are still with us. Every time we recite the creed that says, "I believe in the communion of saints," I think of my great-aunt who once sat where I now sit.

And please do not accuse us of worshiping the building. It is not the building we worship; it is the roots the building represents. All around us are change and decay. The house where I was born is now the site of a filling station; the school where I was educated will educate no one else, for it has been replaced by a parking lot. Yet the small church remains and, as long as it does, it is our psychological link with the past, showing us Sunday after Sunday that we are not adrift. And that sense of not drifting is also shown in our love of order.

Allow me to describe that love with an analogy. In John's Gospel, Jesus' garment is described as a seamless robe. To weave it, its makers had to put every thread in a certain place. Think of people as threads, and you will have the picture of what I mean. If you still do not understand, let me take you back to our now famous women's meeting, picking it up at the point where you were exhorting us to help with the bills.

Susan: Old Jim Clancy might help.
Anne: I would not call him old. He is getting ready to marry for the third time.
Everybody: He is!
Susan: Where are his children? He had a big family.
Anne: The oldest girl got married last year and now has a young boy of her own. Young Jim is after a master's degree in engineering, and his wife is working in a library. Larry, the third boy, is in the army. And Amy, the youngest girl . . .
Pastor: For heaven's sake, what has all this to do with the budget?

That conversation, Reverend, was not for heaven's sake, but for ours. If we have a deep regard for the past, we also have a certain way of looking at the present—a certain social way. We like to know things about our fellow parishioners. Do not put that habit down to idle curiosity. In our scheme of things everybody has a place, and nobody is really happy unless he or she knows that place. You can see that truth in many different ways. Why do we always choose the same pew? Why do we take communion, Sunday after Sunday, in almost the same order? Why do we reelect people to the same offices year after year? It is because of our basic need for social order. You see, we had to discuss Jim Clancy's matrimonial adventures because we had to fit him into our church life. We fitted him in because we love him.

Once, long ago, I was a church school teacher, and the course I taught was called "Our Family the Church." That title captures the essence of my last point. Remember how puzzled you were when we took up a collection to help Pat Jones pay his lawyers? Of course, he was guilty—we all knew that—but he was our guilty parishioner. Pat had grown up in the parish, attended its church school, and sung in its choir. He belonged! Once you belong, we do not desert you. In small churches bonds of affection run deep. In a small parish like ours, unlike a large church, nobody is anonymous. A funeral, a baptism, a wedding are church events that bring all of us to the service because these concern members of our church family. There is no better way to describe us than the verse from Romans which says "None of us lives to himself, and none of us dies to himself."

Obviously, my "three loves" stand in contrast to the way pastors often think. Our love of the past conflicts frequently with your plans for the future; our love of order does not show up on abstract statistics; our tendency to look to each other for affection and support stands against a minister's desire to obtain emotional help away from the small church. The clergy never really belong to a small church; because of that we have a hard time trusting them.

But more than that, we are reluctant to change to your standards. Certainly we want new families, if these people will really understand us. Can we be sure that they will learn and appreciate our long past? Will they realize that we

35

cannot fit them into our structure until we know a good deal about them? Above everything else, will they be willing to be adopted into our parish family and in the process grasp that we are family, with all that word implies in terms of loyalty, care, and love?

The demands a small church places on its membership are high indeed and may seem at first glance to have little to do with Christian love and discipline. Yet, on the other hand, did not Christ form a family that we know as his disciples? Is not love considered one of the highest of Christian virtues? If we were not the way we are, those Christian attributes would and could not exist.

The greatest poem in the English language was written, so Milton said, in order to explain the ways of God to man. This letter hardly meets the standards of *Paradise Lost*, but it is my sincere hope that it may explain the pastor to the small church and the small church to the pastor.

Your loving friend,
Mary Walsh

# IV

## Saying Everything That Is Necessary? That Is Not Christian!

I have decided to write . . . to give you distinct knowledge about the matters of which you have been informed. (The Gospel of Luke)

Canterbury Street
Palestine, Michigan

Dear Paul,

Your question and my reply are worth quoting directly.

"Dean Upchurch, how do you write a weekly religious column for a small-town newspaper?"

"It is easy, Paul. First, spread a lot of blank paper on the floor. Having secured a stout rope you next tie one end to your ankles. Then toss the other end of the rope over a handy beam. Securing the free end, pull yourself into a firm upside-down position directly over the paper. Proceed to bite your tongue quite hard in order to secure a good quantity of blood. After steadying yourself with both hands, you then proceed to write, using your blood as the ink and the sharp end of your nose as the pen."

Well . . . all right . . . I did exaggerate just a bit. But not by much. If you do not believe me, observe my struggles this week to compose a written word or two about the problem of profanity in a small town. After several false starts, my first effort came out like this.

37

## Thou Shalt Not Take the Name of the Lord Thy God in Vain

Have you seen the film *Saturday Night Fever*? Don't bother unless you have three dollars to spare and are interested in the collapse of the English language. To say nothing about the ability to think. Nobody can deny that the movie is an accurate picture of the way many boys and girls talk in the large cities of America. At first, the entire reaction of middle-class America must be one of shock. Still, on reflection, there is a more alarming problem. This movie producer is glorifying an inability to reason. For, you see, people swear because they do not think.

In the production, the foul language does manage to keep the dialogue afloat and give the setting a feeling of authenticity; toss out the four-letter words, and there would be no reason for the film's existence. The power of the language conceals the emptiness of the entire movie.

To say that we who live in this small town are free from this type of talk is to deny one of the most obvious facts of our existence. Indeed, one can hear the words used in *Saturday Night Fever* any time of the day on any of the streets of Palestine. Our community is full of individuals who are mentally lazy.

In reality that is all profanity is—mental laziness. Few of us really wish God to damn a motor that will not start or send to hell a finger we have recently cut. For the moment, we allow our emotions to control our thinking; and we cannot create an appropriate saying. Consequently, we curse.

Thus, after considering the matter further, *Saturday Night Fever* might be worth a visit. It will remind us that socially shocking words are not substitutes for thinking.

I showed this piece of prose to my editor, and he liked it. So did the local Lutheran pastor. Nevertheless, I refused to have it printed. For you see, it has a fatal flaw.

Examine it with care; it becomes a small sermon. Many people in this area stay away from church services and thus away from sermons. My column is written for that type of individual—for the one who deliberately ignores the worship of God week after week. How can I give this person a jolt about his use of profanity? Let us examine our nonattender of church services a little more closely.

Like everybody else, Mr. and Mrs. Nonattender want to be accepted by others in the town. Truthfully, it goes even farther than that—they want to be liked by as many people as possible. Second, it is highly probable that they have not seen *Saturday Night Fever* and that they will not. Last of all, Mr. and Mrs. Nonattender have likely been disappointed in some person at some time because of that individual's behavior. Keep all those elements in mind as you examine my next effort on this theme of avoiding profanity.

## Thou Shalt Not Take the Name of the Lord Thy God in Vain

She was one of those people whom adolescent boys adore—that Miss Angelica Caritas. A dozen times her face and voice had come to me from the screen of the Bijou Theater in such productions as *Scarlet Sands* and *God's Country and the Woman*. Never would I have thought to have seen her in the flesh; yet there she was, resplendent in white blouse and shorts, standing before the counter of my father's grocery store.

"Boy, I am just dying to have some fresh fruit. Could you deliver a box of strawberries to the hotel? They don't have any, but they told me they would prepare a dish if you would send some over."

"Why ... why ... yes!" The proximity of so much loveliness was making me stammer. "Of course ... right away." In a moment the vision of Hollywood was gone, leaving me in absolute rapture. What a story to tell the football team in the locker room! I decided I would begin in quite a casual fashion. "You see, fellows, I was in the middle of dumping some potatoes when ..."

My father, however, was less impressed. In fact, you might say that he was cold to the entire idea.

"Why didn't you get the money?"

"You don't ask Hollywood stars for money, Dad. They have people who take care of things like that."

"I don't care if she's Eleanor Roosevelt, Wallis Simpson, and the Queen of England all rolled into one. If she doesn't pay, she doesn't get any strawberries from me. So collect the cash, or bring them back!"

"If you can't trust Miss Caritas with all her money, whom can you trust?" I muttered under my breath. "Perhaps she has a charge account at the hotel." The thought dispelled my despair. "Sure, I'll just ask Dolly for the money ..."

But Dolly, the desk clerk, dashed my hope.

"We ain't paying nothing to nobody." Dolly glared at me from behind thick glasses. "You'll have to collect from the goddess herself."

I gulped, but finally managed to ask where Miss Caritas was.

"Out back," snorted Dolly, jerking an ink-stained finger toward a swinging door. Then she placed a fat hand on a fatter hip. "She's holding court for every buck in the hotel. You can stand in line with the rest of them."

Sure enough, Miss Caritas, dressed in a two-piece green outfit, was lying on the grass and surrounded by several lovesick males. A pause that followed a roar of laughter gave me a chance to break into the conversation.

"Here are your strawberries, Miss Caritas."

"Take them to the kitchen, boy."

"I'm afraid . . . I mean . . . You see, my father wants the money for them now." My face twitched with embarrassment.

"Okay, get it at the hotel desk."

"Well . . . I'm afraid that Dolly will not give it to me." My stomach felt like lead. "But I'm sure you can straighten things out." I smiled weakly.

Miss Caritas rolled over, swiftly got on all fours, and looked me square in the face. It suddenly occurred to me that she looked just like my mother cat getting ready to join battle.

"You tell that fat @#§%&*%&! sloppy desk clerk to pay up or I will have her head!" The voice of the goddess rose to a shrill crescendo. "And once more tell that kitchen staff to get that fruit prepared fast!" Expletives and curses flowed from the mouth of my beloved.

I gasped and fled with the strawberries.

From time to time my lady parishioners tell me that Miss Caritas is still active on daytime television. She plays the part of a sweet old grandmother on "Dark Abyss." Her counter character is a young girl—her granddaughter, I believe—who is rebellious and always ready to violate social courtesy and customs. It is the task of Miss Caritas to straighten her granddaughter out. Again . . . this is what my lady parishioners tell me. I really do not not know, for I never watch. I am too afraid that I might laugh.

Thou Shalt Not Take the Name of the Lord Thy God in Vain.


Here is a parable and not a sermon. Parables are easier to remember than sermons—especially if the story teaches us the advantages of Christian behavior in our present social setting. I do not deny that frequently one's religion does get in

41

the way of town and local custom; but, when social norms and Christian behavior happen to coincide, there is no reason why one's writing should not take advantage of the fact.

Leaving my efforts for this week and going to a broader theme, I feel that too many writers of religious columns do not strive hard enough for freshness and imagination. Interpreted, that means hard work. In his book *The Elements of Style*, E. B. White emphasizes that fact. Often I rewrite a paragraph five or six times before I am certain that it says clearly what I want it to say. Although I carry a little notebook with me at all times so that I can jot down ideas for my column, those ideas must be expressed in a way that people can clearly understand. Therefore, before you begin to write, make sure that you have a dictionary and a thesaurus within easy reach of your typewriter.

Forgive me if I refrain from more advice; I am beginning to sound too much like a sixth-grade English teacher. In truth, I would rather outline my struggles with this week's religious column than list a series of methods. Every person who wishes to write must learn his own way. In plain English, Paul, the best way to learn the art of writing is to do it.

With all good wishes,
A. M. Upchurch, Dean

# V

# Hey, Reverend!
# Why Isn't the Women's Washroom Cleaner?

"The horror of the moment," the King went on, "I shall never, never forget!"
"You will though," the Queen said, "if you don't make a memorandum of it." (Lewis Carroll—*Through the Looking Glass*)

10 Church Street
Bypass, Michigan

Dear Pastor,

From the tales various women of the parish have been telling me, it sounds as if yesterday's church service was very exciting. Of course, I am not referring to the liturgy or to your sermon, but rather to the confrontation between you and Joy Jones, the current president of the Women's Guild. Anne was on the telephone bright and early and just full of information when she discovered that I was back in town! From what she told me (and her facts have been supplemented by several other people), you were standing at the door greeting your parishioners when Joy presented herself. To your "Good morning," she replied, "It *would* be a good morning, if you kept the washrooms cleaner!" According to Anne, you next stated, "It is not my task to clean them!" Back came Joy with, "Old Reverend Arnold used to keep them spotless!" You retorted, "Saint Thomas

Aquinas didn't spend his time cleaning bathrooms!". That really poured coal on the fire! Eventually the warden had to break up the argument by summoning you downstairs to check the church furnace.

Now, I do not know whether or not the angelic doctor spent time looking after washrooms, but since that great boon to Western civilization—the American public restroom—had not yet been invented, I don't suppose that he did. What I do know, however, is that I am going to have to take care of Joy at the next meeting of the Women's Guild; and, frankly, I am not looking forward to it. During my seventy years, I have seen many a confrontation between clergy and the women of the church, and good seldom came out of any of these arguments. In this present hullabaloo, I do not know who is right and who is wrong. In the long run that will not matter. What does matter to me is that the parish may pay a lasting penalty for this sort of nonsense. So, if you don't mind—and even if you do—I would like a few minutes of your time to explain some of the reasons why this Women's Guild exists and works in the way it does.

To begin, a clergyman frequently sees an association of church women as a sort of supplement to the main church budget. It is to this group that he goes when there is a need for a new furnace or for a new sidewalk or for a new rectory stove. Women are also handy when it comes time to cook the annual father-daughter banquet or organize a vacation Bible school. In short, he often sees their value as an organization in terms of work. Ladies, however, are likely to have a far different set of values, and these values may have little to do with a pastor's ideas.

An illustration here may be helpful. I am old enough to remember the Depression and to remember it as a time when women's work in the diocese flourished. It may come as a surprise to you, but in those days Saint Stephen's had neither a regular pastor nor a regular worship service. What we did have was the Women's Guild—and an order from the bishop to shut everything down. The guild met for prayer, for Bible study, and for money-raising projects. It turned out that the people within the group cared little for suggestions from the outside. Why was this? Simple enough—the members of the guild looked upon themselves as the church! That is an attitude that is far from dead even now. If faced with this statement, most members of the guild would, of course, deny it; but don't let that fool you. Quickly enough you will see what I mean when you try to alter their thinking by quoting from the Bible or from a memo from diocesan headquarters!

Now, this point of view leads to certain interesting ramifications. The guild may well become a church within a church. Do not be surprised if the organization embarks on projects without consulting you and the vestry. Again, do not be unhappy when you come to the members with a suggestion and they turn you down. Like all institutions, the instinct of the Women's Guild is to preserve its money and its power. Sometimes the two get a bit confused! A friend of mine, the wife of an Episcopal pastor, once summed it all by saying, "Women's groups are seldom amenable to indirect suggestions from the clergy and are even less in favor of direct ones!" Still believe it or not—there are ways of influencing this group.

The key to the entire situation, dear Pastor, lies with the clergyperson who understands the forces that bring women together into church groups in the first place and keeps them there. You may be under the impression that these forces are theological and spiritual, and to some extent that is true; but there is another element that is even more important.

Contrary to much popular thinking, most women value another woman's friendship. This is especially true among those who form your current church's guild. Consequently, these ladies, although they may care little for the pros and cons of the argument between you and Joy, will be anxious to placate her because they wish to lose neither her friendship

45

nor her membership. Again, she belongs to the "family compact" of Bypass and is ruthless enough to take advantage of that social position. Believe me, she is going to come to the next meeting of the church women loaded for bear!

Yet, Joy, in the long run, will seek a compromise. Many of the members are tired of her attempts to trade on her social and economic position; and Joy, not being stupid, knows it. Most of her friends are in the guild, and in her turn she will not wish to lose their friendship. That could well happen if she goes too far. You see, we know her and she knows that we know her. When she runs out of steam, Joy will turn positive and make some statement about the guild's hiring a janitor (which we cannot afford) or creating a volunteer work schedule (which nobody will keep). I shall back her up, and then—and not until then—I shall trot out your good points. Anxious to make peace, everybody will agree that you are a fine fellow, but very inexperienced. I am afraid that all this will be hard on your ego, but remember there is no public record of what each member thinks privately. Anyway, there is more at stake here than your pride. In order to function well, the members of the guild must see that their friendship to each other is no longer threatened by a parish dispute that might force them to take sides. Allow that bond to be cemented again, and you will be in a position to exercise your leadership. Now, how can that be accomplished?

The local guild is cemented by its friendship. It also decides things and moves on those decisions. Occasionally, in a small church, if the pastor is personable and has been there a long time, he may be the chief activator. This, however, will be very rare. Women are much more likely to listen to another woman than they are to the clergy, and this is especially true when the woman is a shaper of opinion. Note that I said "a shaper of opinion" and not an "action-maker." "Opinion-makers" and "action-makers" may be the same people, but do not count on it. Often "opinion-makers" prefer the background. They may not even come to meetings, but rest assured that they will be consulted before any major decisions are made. The trick in communicating with a women's organization is to consult with the "opinion-makers" before you do anything else. If the "opinion-makers" say no (and you will be surprised at the number of times they will say yes), do not press the issue. If you do, you will run the danger of being defeated; and a clergyman cannot run the risk of being defeated too often. Drop the matter for a time and then try another strategy to obtain it. But—back to the theme of this section. How do you spot the "opinion-makers"? As I stated above it is not always easy, so here are a few rules that may prove helpful.

1. Whom do the members mention most often with approval?
2. What women belong to your oldest and best established families?
3. What women have been members of the guild for the longest time?
4. What women belong to families that shape and run this small town of Bypass, Michigan?

Frequently, one woman may fit several of these categories; and, if she does, her influence in the guild is probably greater than yours or the vestry's. Cultivate her carefully!

Despite all that I have said, the members of Saint Stephen's parish will recognize that there are certain things expected of them, and probably they will do them. Every fall we always hold a bazaar, every winter we always hold a bake sale, and every spring we sponsor a church supper. On the surface it looks as if these activities are designed for the sole purpose of raising money. Before passing that judgment, however, let us look a little more beneath the surface. This is a deliberate step on my part because there is a strong feeling in this denomination that these money-making projects should be abolished and everybody encouraged to tithe. Heaven knows, I have nothing against tithing! I have done it myself for years, but there are other considerations when we come to the activities of the guild. The truth of the matter is that neither you nor the bishop could stop the women of this parish from holding all the money-raising projects they wish to put on. It may come as a surprise; but I assure you that most of the members of the guild, despite all the moans and groans about the work involved, do want these types of activities. For one thing, if these projects were not held, the group would lose part of its purpose; and all organizations need a purpose. Second, money is a goal that is easily measured, understood, and appreciated. In addition, bazaars and suppers give many people the opportunity to show their skills, to be appreciated, and to fit into the life of the parish. Last of all, to take some of these women out of the kitchen or away from the craft table is to deprive them of a skill they do best. Not everybody in the church can read in public or teach children or be a spokesperson at a meeting. Those who lack these abilities still need the chance to express their faith by demonstrating what they can do with their hands.

Pastor, I am the last of a breed—a retired Latin teacher! Nobody wants to learn that language anymore, despite the fact that many a Roman author had a view of life that was extremely penetrating. Among them was the poet Virgil, who believed that life was essentially cyclical. In plain English, he thought things repeated themselves. Much as I admire Virgil, I do not believe that. As far as your dealings with the guild are concerned, however, he will probably prove his point unless everybody involved learns to trust each other, value each other, and above all . . . to love each other.

Your loving friend,
Mary Walsh

48

# VI

# Whom Do I Love?
# Why You, Reverend!

A baited mousetrap does not make you into the mouse. (Old Surrey Saying)

Jubilee Seminary
Collegetown, U.S.A.

Dear Paul,

May sex be blessed . . . and cursed as far as the clergy are concerned! Your epistle about Mrs. X arrived this morning; and, to say the least, it has occupied most of my waking hours until now. From your guarded language, I am certain that her husband did and does have good reason for his jealousy and bad temper—despite Mrs. X's naive assumption that wedding vows are medieval and out of date. I applaud your efforts to educate her on those commitments; but, the serious nature of the situation notwithstanding, I did permit myself to laugh. Really, Paul, there is a good deal about the world that you have not yet grasped, although you did receive an inkling when Mrs. X told you that she "wanted a chance to express her affection for you in a more realistic way"! Now, I have heard of styles and styles in this kind of thing, but I must confess this is a new approach.

However, let not panic sit at your door, for this story is as old as the church (remember the problems of Saint Anthony!)—and as new as the next crop of seminary

49

graduates. Often have I heard your dean state that "clergypersons are targets," and nowhere does it apply better than to your present difficulties. Many a pastor has admitted to me that he has experienced the same sort of opportunity—or hazard—as you. It is also interesting to note that women clergy are also experiencing this same type of annoyance. Just last month one of our recent feminine graduates came by and told me that she was having difficulties with a male parishioner; indeed, if one switches the sex of the counselor and the counselee, your two situations would be almost congruent. I must add that she was almost as distraught as you about the happening, and it might be interesting for both of you to compare notes and see what type of a solution you could create for this type of upset. Yet, that will take time, and so I shall offer some observations and solutions for the present. Thus, to business!

First of all, you did what you should have done—go to some experienced individual for aid. Reactions to this situation must be clearly thought through before any action is taken. To be loved by another person of the opposite sex is one of life's main goals and you have reached it. You would be a rare person if you did not feel a sense of accomplishment—and a sense of pride. Consequently, to be able to think straight under such circumstances would be extremely difficult.

And, above all else, straight thinking is required. Is there not much more involved than you and Mrs. X? Are there not modern philosophies working that see this happening as fortuitous? Twenty years ago, I would not have begun this letter by even hinting that you and Mrs. X might consummate her desires, but now I no longer dare to omit guidance on this piece of Christian teaching. In truth, there are counselors who would advise the lady—providing you could be persuaded—to proceed to ultimate satisfaction for the sake of her mental health. The one condition laid down in this matter is "discretion." When I hear these counselors, I am always tempted to ask their definition of "discretion." Surely, they cannot mean an action taken with careful prudence in order to avoid risk or danger! What is prudent about risking a marriage and your career in a small community whose inhabitants are probably specialists in watching their neighbors? There are also family members who would be very embarrassed should this type of relationship surface. And then we have . . . the church! When I say "the church," I mean an institution that stands for certain teachings. You, like many tempted pastors, are in a position to do it a great deal of harm if you break any of its rules. Given these facts, would not "discretion" dictate that you and Mrs. X forego any plans to consummate the bliss? Pastor, you can answer the question!

There is another side to the question which, as we shall see, Mrs. X may not be capable of considering. This is the role of your conscience. Somehow the attempt of modern biblical scholars to lessen the sinful aspects of adultery and fornication do not ring true to those times or to these. Indeed, I can never think of these arguments without going back in my own mind to my parish and a rather painful scene with a woman parishioner of mine who had remained with her husband through two of his infidelities, but could not bear the thought of a third. At the close of one very brutal hour, she turned to me and asked, "Pastor, can a marriage die spiritually?" Being young, I denied it; but now I am convinced that it can happen. From all my hours of listening to people, I can assure you that there is nothing that lays the ax to the roots of marriage faster than infidelity. Rationally, I have never understood it; but here you are dealing, not with reason, but with emotion. This comes out very clearly in modern literature and song through "I want to give myself to you" or "I do not care whether it is right or wrong." Whatever else you can say, these are highly charged expressions. Do you suppose that things were any the less electric when husband and wife first plighted their troth? In plain truth, a

Christian cannot love without mixing accountability with the emotions—no matter what your lady assumes. Consequently, let us dismiss Mrs. X's wishes from our field of possibilities.

What then exists within the range of the practical? In the course of years, I have had at least a dozen pastors come to me with this problem; and I always tell them to begin by reading Saint Peter on the subject. In his first letter, Peter, it is true, was striving to strengthen his followers against persecution, not sexual temptation; but the advice pertains to either situation.

"Keep," says Saint Peter, "your conscience clear, so that, when you are insulted, those who speak evil of your good conduct as followers of Christ may be made ashamed of what they say."

"Keep your conscience clear!" How sound that recommendation is to all Christian pastors, no matter what the circumstances. In the final analysis, it will be this guide that has to tell you what to do and how to do it; in other words, know your own inner motivations and how to express them when next you interview Mrs. X.

We know how Mrs. X defines "love"—to her it is the same as lust—but it is interesting that when Saint Paul deals with the subject in 1 Corinthians 13 he does not bother with fixed limits. Rather, he tells us how true affection really works. Again, the saint couches much of his language in verbal forms—in other words, he wants the concept to be active and not passive. Be prepared then to make your views toward the proposition quite certain. Nevertheless, there is no need for this last meeting to degenerate into a shouting match in which you demonstrate either real or feigned anger. As far as you are concerned, you are still the pastor—still the leader who has control of the situation and wishes it to move in a certain direction. And what would this be? Well, frankly, your usefulness in this relationship is finished—or nearly so. Everybody who engages in counseling has to know the limits of his effectiveness, and you have almost reached it. Your one remaining objective with this woman is to anchor her in another parish and with another counselor and to do it with kindness and firmness.

This may be a difficult assignment; no pastor likes to lose parishioners. In addition, do not overlook the fact that pastors are human, and that means they are susceptible to flattery. In plain Irish, we like blarney as well as the next fellow—even if we know that much of what we are hearing has a false foundation. After all, most of us in this profession aspire to be excellent pastoral counselors and praise from a counselee is attractive. To deal with this type of temptation, I have always considered a healthy knowledge of spiritual categories to be an excellent defense. Therefore, let us consider your client in terms of moral growth; it has long been recognized that the Christian life demands development, although many of the ancient classifications are not entirely understood in our present theological climate.

But—before I begin the descriptions that I feel pertain to your situation, be forewarned! The waters of life run deeper than you or I can ever plumb; an analysis which would reduce every individual soul to one type or another is doomed from the beginning. Clear-cut classifications about virtue and vice may be beloved by preachers, but ultimately they will fail you in the realm of the spirit. Every time I contemplate labeling some person, I always think of Saint Paul—interesting, is it not, that his writings have come up twice in this letter—and his inconstant behavior as a theologian. This man can tell us at one moment that love believes all things and hopes all things, and then in the next breath explain that love and hope are quite separate, but no less abiding, virtues! Despite the intellectual difficulty of seeing where the two moral merits are separate and the same, are not the conditions he outlines true to the Christian life? In short, pastoral counseling—especially when it makes use of great religious ideals—is more of an art than a science.

Why then bother to categorize Mrs. X at all? The answer is easy—because it is useful. Few pastors and fewer parishioners are sufficiently equipped to enter into a deep examination of the human soul; that task should be left to those who are trained to the task. As far as you are concerned personally, you cannot do much more for Mrs. X; that has already been established. Today, the danger to pastoral work lies not in mistaken analysis, but in no moral analysis at all. Much truth has come down to us from well-established Christian writers like Aquinas and Wesley, but to many clergy these truths lie buried in some books that line study shelves. We parsons are much more likely to know the categories of some psychological school than to know a theological description of conscience. This state of affairs is not helped by the fact that we live in a world which does not oppose Christian standards—how could it oppose something that it does not really know?—but has its own philosophy that everybody has the duty to pursue his or her own happiness. The practical result has been a civilization in which morality is no longer considered a matter that God has revealed and man has discovered. And what useful discovery can be put forward? Here, I feel, is the time to introduce the old idea of the "once born" and the "twice born."

Today, there is such an emphasis on the commandment "Ye must be born again" that almost everybody in America, if not the world, has at least a vague idea what is meant by the expression "the twice born." It will suffice for your dealings with Mrs. X to point out that the "twice born" must have a moral sense. Soon you will know whether Mrs. X fits into the category of the "twice born," for her conflicting emotional difficulties will be too much for her to conceal. Religious behavior and sexual passion often struggle—this is one of the most obvious facts of human existence—and thus it is highly likely that if your parishioner is "twice born" that struggle would have surfaced before now. If it should at your next meeting, then you must seize hold of her statements which affirm Christian morality and use them as a basis that will urge her to seek help elsewhere; but, since she seems not at all bothered by her invitation, my guess is that you are dealing with an individual who is "once born." This type of person is difficult to recognize and almost impossible to cure; and, despite my suspicions, I am in no position to make more than a preliminary estimate of her character. You, however—despite the reluctance which I know you must feel—have to make up your own mind about this parishioner of yours. Consequently, my chief remaining role is to set out before you a description of the way the "once born" see themselves, the world, and other people.

Personally, despite my reputation for expecting the worst from everything and everybody, I find "once born" individuals very attractive. I suspect this appeal comes from their romantic way of viewing things; for, although they may know that sin and sickness exist, they pay them little attention. The truly "twice born" have known pessimism and defeat and have been delivered from them; the "once born" are too optimistic to pay these facts any mind, for they are too busy pursuing their own happiness. Theologically, God exists, but only for one purpose—to bring joy and pleasure to as many as possible. Times of stress and personal difficulties are seen as caused by other people or by circumstances over which the "once born" have no control; almost never do they view these happenings as caused by their own defects of character. It follows that their own imperfections cause them not the slightest distress, for they do not realize that they have any. Not infrequently, their romantic turn of mind wishes a more physical expression; and doctors, politicians—and clergy—make excellent marks. Still, I must warn you that, if you decide that Mrs. X belongs to this classification, it would be a waste of time to confront her with what I have just told you; for all she would grasp is the fact that you disapprove of her proposal—she would never understand why you do.

The reason is simple enough; the "once born," even if they

55

attend church regularly, take what they wish from the service and ignore the rest—rather like the patron at a restaurant who orders the sweet dessert first and then, finding himself full, feels justified in ignoring the main course. Human suffering does melt them to tenderness, and they are always ready to take in a stray kitten or feed the hungry parson; but the reasons why the kitten is homeless or the parson is hungry do not interest them. In short, of human sin and of the causes of world shortcomings, they know little and care less; they see the church not as an institution dedicated to getting its hands dirty in the struggle with evil, but as a club whose chief function in life is to promote the happiness of its members.

When these "once born" want something from other people, they have the knack of shoving reality aside and replacing it with rationalizations—sometimes of the most outrageous sort. I am convinced that, if they want something badly enough, most of the "once born" are incapable of distinguishing emotion from thought. "If I feel this way, it must be good," says their mind; and, since they have little or no conscience, they bring social disaster often in their wake. It goes without saying that the "once born," despite their optimistic, sunny outlook on life, can turn out to be a terrible danger to the lonely, unsuspecting pastor.

Do not suppose from my outline that there are more "once born" women than men. When I was a parish parson, I had more than one tearful wife turn to her adulterous or drunken husband and ask, "Is it something I do that makes you do these things?" Almost without fail, the husbands would become irritated or repentant, but there were always a few that had no answer because they could not understand why their wives were objecting to their behavior. To them, the great value of life was the pursuit of their own happiness; why should anybody deny that to them?

Regardless of her rating as "once born" or "twice born," Mrs. X must get out of your life and to another counselor. Probably it would be best if you did the arranging. Choose a man or woman who can be trusted and knows something about people with character defects. Your fellow clergy in Bypass may be a great aid in this selection. Once a new counselor has been selected and Mrs. X chooses to see him or her, the counselor must be told under the seal of professional ethics all you know. This, by the way, includes your opinions; but make sure that you sift opinion from fact. Quoting me is permissible as far as I am concerned, providing you stress the fact that I feel strongly that Mrs. X's husband must be told about her feelings toward you. No marriage can survive under false colors, and few marital problems can be solved without the aid of both partners. Should Mrs. X be "twice born," she will understand that well enough; if she is "once born," the shock of having to face her inner weakness might be just enough to shake her from this infantile moral stance. Possibly you may fear the husband's reaction more than Mrs. X's—even if you are innocent. Remember, however, that, if Mr. X does appear in your study, he will probably not be seeking to convict you, but wishing to find the assurance that you were always the pastor and never the lover.

Last of all, think of yourself. Despite the fact that you have been through a harrowing experience, you have up to the present made no major error. In a very real way you have been introduced to a perpetual problem that seminaries largely ignore, and yet you did not allow this adventure with Mrs. X to destroy you. And I hope that you have learned something about the emotional forces that are present in this world and how they can involve unsuspecting people—all of which a "twice born" individual takes in his stride, for he knows that Christ has overcome the world.

With all good wishes,
Theophilus Ignatius, Principal
Jubilee Seminary

# VII

## To Drink or Not to Drink? Now There Is a Question!

*Abstinence is as easy to me as temperance would be difficult.*
(Hannah More—*Anecdotes of Samuel Johnson*)

10 Church Street
Bypass, Michigan

Dear Pastor,

"Drat anyway," to quote my cousin Elizabeth. Here I am in bed with my cat, a steam kettle, a dose of influenza and . . . a bottle of brandy! No, that last item is not meant as a challenge—although, judging by your pastoral prayer last night at the annual Christmas party of the Bypass Chamber of Commerce, it might seem to be. Your old nemesis, Joy Jones, dropped in to check on my pulse, my consumption of brandy, and the state of the house and to make sure that I was well informed about all the happenings last evening. From what she told me, I have gathered that you asked God to thwart everything from "a" to "y"—at any rate you implored him to stop people at the party from drinking to the point where they might commit adultery or Yuletide excess. Of course, Joy enjoyed the whole business immensely—I have always thought that she missed her vocation by not going to Hollywood and becoming a gossip columnist—but I, like a certain English queen, am not amused. Only saddened! Since I have seen you take a drink,

58

my first reaction was that of anger. Were you being hypocritical? Then a saner mood descended as I considered your personality, until at last I came to the conclusion that you, like so many others, are simply confused about the consumption of alcohol. How I wish I could rise from my bed and have a face-to-face confrontation with you on the subject, but my wobbly walking state—caused by the flu, I assure you, and not the brandy—makes that a forlorn wish. Still, one side of me is disgusted and angry with you; I expected a much better and more sensible approach from you on this subject. I am no prude, and I am not a sociologist. My only qualifications for taking you to task are those of an individual who learned her trade by reading the Bible and other religious classics in the original tongue and who has spent most of her life observing the behavior of people in a small town—especially their behavior toward spirituous liquor.

In a way this entire thing is ridiculous. Here I am, an old Latin and Greek teacher, discussing with a young clergyman one of the most explosive issues in the church. Most spiritual leaders never bother to deal with the subject—except to praise abstinence. Therefore, why should I be bothered to compose this letter? The only justification I can find is that despite all the talk, fiery sermons, and defiant actions that surround alcohol the average small-town parson and the average small-town layman do not know much about the subject. Have you ever heard a discussion or a sermon that actually taught you about the nature of liquor and laid down certain rules about its consumption? I never have; and yet, as a young person, I would have welcomed a chance to know, should I choose to drink, how to handle it. Most of the information given out on the subject deals with the alcoholic, but I am not an alcoholic and most of my friends are not alcoholics. We drink socially because we like to do it; but nobody, as far as I know, ever taught one of my acquaintances how to use liquor in a responsible fashion.

In this country we do not teach people to deal with the issue in a sensible fashion because we have surrounded it with misconceptions, a great many myths, and almost total guilt. To many of us, a drunken individual is a figure of fun—"Hold the house steady, wife, while I fit the key into the lock!"—when in reality he is a sick person in desperate need of help. A good percentage of us think quite earnestly that social drinking is likely to lead to alcoholism, although most of my friends who drink liquor do not fit into that category. Americans surround hard drink with many laws, customs, and taboos that make its consumption, not a natural thing known to man since the dawn of history, but something attractive because it is dangerous and, in many of our minds, immoral.

Do not suppose that I am arguing that everybody should drink alcohol! I do believe that you can make out a strong case for total abstinence and also a strong case for what I call "accountable drinking." Where most people make a mistake is that they never decide which course they should follow. In essence, they make a third choice—what I designate as the "sense of drift." The "sense of drift" can take over many parts of a person's life; it pertains to more than alcohol, believe me! We accept the "sense of drift" because it follows the easiest road. As far as alcohol is concerned, dismiss the "sense of drift" as a possible course of action. Those who are cast into the role of community leader should leave nothing to chance, especially if that "nothing to chance" can be dangerous to society, to their careers, and to their souls.

Are you tired of my lecture? Do you want to rip this entire letter to shreds and tell me to mind my own business? One moment, Reverend Sir, before you consign me and my message to perdition! In small communities, people have their own peculiar reasons for taking a great deal of interest in how the average parson deals with alcohol. Like it or not, Americans have inherited a historical situation on this subject, and its influence is still mighty. A good many citizens of Bypass assume that no good Christian could keep a tavern and no tavernkeeper could be a Christian. False that judgment is; but, given what has been preached from many pulpits, I am certain that you can appreciate how that attitude arose. There are still individuals—especially those who wear a blue collar—who grade people's religiosity by the amount of liquor he does not consume. In their thinking, when you are "saved" you must cease to drink wine or other spirits. And should not all clergymen be "saved"? For this and other reasons, many inhabitants of country communities, whether they belong to a church or not, will be interested in your attitude toward strong drink and will almost automatically measure you by the way you deal with it. Do not assume that people regard your consumption of alcohol as a sin—that is not always true—but always understand that you are being monitored on the subject. This dimension of your activity (or nonactivity) will be noted by many who would never dream of entering Saint Stephen's parish church for regular worship Unfortunately, clergypersons in small towns are targets on this and other bugaboos. Many a farmer has justified his drunkenness to his wife by saying, "Well, even the old Reverend takes a drink!" In all probability the "old Reverend" never became intoxicated in his life, but a wife confronted with an inebriated spouse may not bother to make the distinction between one drink and many—especially if she believes that it is always wrong to consume liquor.

In all fairness, people belonging to this way of thinking do have strong arguments. To go over the statistics that link excessive drinking to family problems and automobile accidents would be a wearying task, but that does not make those statistics less relevant to our Bypass lives. You need not look far in order to see the power of alcohol in Bypass or any other small town. How well can it be understood that certain individuals choose never to accept liquor! It is my private conviction—something which I hope everybody will come to share—that abstainers deserve the highest respect.

Thus, if you ever become a teetotaler, I shall fully understand and appreciate your position. Please, however, a cautious word! In every small town there are people who never consume liquor and manage things so that everybody knows about it promptly—which may be all right. Then they put every person on the defensive—which is all wrong. I speak from sad experience, remembering well the time I attended a temperance meeting. When the speaker invited questions I—rather brashly—asked him what new laws were being prepared and what new plans were being formulated to make the sale of liquor illegal, since obviously the present ones were not working. Upset, the speaker came down from the platform, shouted loud and long, and reinforced each one of his statements by banging his fist down on the end of a handy pew. This type of behavior—what I call the Carrie Nation Approach—does the cause of total abstinence more harm than good. If, out of a personal conviction, you decide never to consume alcohol, I trust that you can be assertive about your decision in a moderate fashion. Often people in small towns have sensitive antennae when it comes to clergy and alcohol. My mother would never admit any pastor to her house unless he had telephoned first; she wanted to make sure that her wine and wine glasses were well concealed! Do your testimony by action and avoid dramatic scenes. And if possible . . . never, never antagonize!

In all fairness one can understand why opponents to alcohol often become frustrated and angry; constantly, they are surrounded by what they dislike. All brands of liquor are advertised on television, sold in grocery stores, and dispensed by the glass over the entire United States. Such a contiguous relationship is bound to make many abstainers quite uncomfortable and seem like one long challenge. Consequently, it is not surprising that crusaders against strong drink will sometimes make their position clear in less than temperate language and actions, hoping to influence others to follow their lead. Personally, I wonder just how effective such a witness is. The abstainers, I know—and I have met quite a few—have come to their position because they have misused alcohol or because they have seen others misuse it. As I see it, people who really want to witness will do best by demonstrating their own control over all phases of their lives. Human nature is a perverse thing, often difficult to master and even more difficult to influence. Know and correct yourself first before you try to correct others.

Have I been fair to the position of the total abstainer? I cannot tell with certainty; for I have lived otherwise. I see alcohol as part of God's creation, something that is basically good, but which, like so many other things, can be corrupted by man. Psalm 104 states that God created wine in order to gladden the hearts of men. Jesus obviously used the juice of the grape. Most biblical passages that deal with strong drink seem to treat its consumption as something natural. Indeed, we know that wine was drunk extensively all over the ancient world because of the foul state of the water. What the Bible does not like—and what no Christian should like—is drunkenness. As I have stated, I respect those who choose never to drink alcohol; and I agree with them that inebriation is to be avoided, but . . . I reserve my own right to follow my own position on the matter. Oddly enough, despite what I have just written, my beginning thesis is quite negative in tone; for it states that the chief problem with liquor in America is that the average American does not know how to drink!

Startling as that last statement is, I am quite sure that I can prove it. In this country do we not see liquor as something that enables us to "let off steam" or "to unwind"? From childhood many individuals see strong drink as something special, when in reality it is one of the most common things known to man. Almost never do we take time to learn how to use it sensibly, despite many people's education in its misuse. We dislike individuals who do not have proper table manners, but we often tolerate those who do not use common sense when they consume alcohol. Why is this so? Simple enough—many people have never been taught a few rules about drinking alcohol. Consequently what should bring pleasure often leads to pain.

Among my talents is the ability to blow up rocks and stumps with dynamite. I learned to use this explosive on my father's farm when we were clearing land for new fruit trees. I used dynamite quite well because I had respect for its power; I have used liquor for over fifty years and never became drunk because I also had a good respect for its power. In a way the two products are parallel; they are both useful, dangerous, and explosive. Do not use either of them if you do not know the regulations that govern their use. I did not blow up stumps when I was angry; I do not drink when I am frustrated or anxious. A person who tries to correct his emotions by making a big bang can inflict a dangerous injury to his body: an individual who drinks to relieve some internal pain may well discover that the cure is worse than the disease. First and foremost—never allow emotions to dictate the amount of liquor you are consuming.

Then you should understand your product. The amount of alcohol in a bottle is often referred to as a "proof." Two hundred proof is raw alcohol; 100 proof means that the contents contain a liquid that is one-half alcohol. In plain English, divide the "proof" by two in order to obtain the percentage of the alcohol. Note also that liquor is both a drug and a food. It is also a liquid that can be rapidly absorbed into the human system. Your body deals with it through the process of regular digestion and can manage quite well—providing it is not overloaded. For most of who are not alcoholics, this means that we can safely drink one and one-half ounces of unmixed alcohol if we spread it out over a twelve-hour day. Thus, whenever you buy liquor you should be careful never to call for a martini or an Old-Fashioned without specifying the exact amount of alcohol it should contain. For example, the average social drinker should be able to absorb three drinks containing not more than one ounce of 100 proof alcohol between noon and midnight on any given day. Personally, no matter what the occasion, I always make sure that at least one hour has passed since my last drink before I even think of having another.

Again, I never indulge unless I have eaten first; and I never have a party at which I serve liquor without making sure that my guests have ready access to some food. There are two commonsense reasons for this. In the United States, as I have said, we see alcohol frequently as something special instead of being a sustenance. Thus, serving it with food may help get the entire business back into perspective. Second, food will absorb your strong drink and put a layer between the liquor and your stomach wall, slowing down the speed at which the alcohol is absorbed.

To repeat, I am not suggesting that everybody immediately take up the habit of eating three times between 12:00 P.M. and 12:00 A.M. and washing everything down with three drinks that contain no more than one ounce of alcohol! The decision must be yours and ought to be based on the facts, your own personality, and the theology of your church. "Accountable drinking" means just that. Since my earliest introduction to alcohol, I have made the way I deal with it a part of my rule of life. If I break any regulations about this matter, I end up in trouble with myself, my Christian values, my conscience, and my God! In turn, I have to make a confession, do penance, ask for forgiveness, and then pray frequently and specifically to the Lord that he will help me stick to my rule of life.

Why then do I consume it at all? As both my body and my influenza germ can testify, it can make me feel more comfortable when I am ill. In moderate amounts it is an aid to communication and good fellowship; I am certain that this is one of the reasons it has been used so extensively by nearly all the people in the world, despite all the social and family problems it has helped to cause. I am careful never to drink alone; to be truthful I enjoy the company of Joy more than the drinks we have together during my battles with influenza. Should I ever begin to look on alcohol as an end in itself, I trust that I will have the good sense to leave it alone.

Since I have given you my own personal philosophy and my own personal regulations about liquor, I might as well add a footnote. It comes from my father. This gentleman was always careful about his dress, the company he kept, and where he was seen—especially where he was seen. Once, after some friends and I had engaged in a little "Detroit slumming," he summed up his feelings about our expedition in one succinct question. "Why," asked he, "deal with the worst when you can get what you want from the best?" Why, indeed? There are certain restaurants in Bypass that can serve food with their drinks—remember that point?—are brightly lit; act like they are not ashamed of what they are doing; and, most important of all, will not damage your prestige when you are seen entering them. Places that dispense liquor in Bypass are closely observed by a great many people. They are places of interest because, although strong drink is readily obtainable in most small towns, a lot of them have an uneasy conscience over that fact. If you doubt that statement, go down to city hall and observe how many bylaws are concerned with its regulation. To add to the difficulty, we citizens of Bypass carefully classify liquor outlets on a scale from "shouldn't be seen in one" to "an excellent drinking establishment." This grading has a habit of rubbing off on the establishment's clientele. No clergyman can hide in a small town; citizens will note your presence almost everywhere you go. So . . . think carefully and have a good reason before you enter any poorly run liquor emporium. Habituating such a place will destroy your position in Bypass faster than anything else I can think of.

Bah, anyway! I feel like Saint Paul dispensing advice to Timothy—"Take a little wine for the sake of your stomach!" I have said enough; perhaps too much! There are a great many things in small towns that cannot guide your conscience; but in the final analysis that will not matter, for heaven is supposed to be the power that teaches us to behave. Yet, does not a conscience grow? Given the strong feelings many clergy have about strong drink, I trust that you will always be true to God's will on this matter. Emotions ought not to get in the way of your actions; if you find that they do—then leave alcohol alone. However, if you can see alcohol as one of God's gifts that can bring pleasure, providing its consumption is carefully regulated, then you are free to use it or to leave it alone. Either way you can serve as an example of Christian witness. And after all, that is one of your chief tasks in Bypass, Michigan.

Your loving friend,
Mary Walsh

# VIII

## The Patients Are So Hopeful

O God . . . make us, we pray, deeply aware of the shortness and uncertainty of human life and let your Holy Spirit lead us in holiness and righteousness all our days. (Jeremy Taylor)

Canterbury Street
Palestine, Michigan

Dear Paul,

Would you share a decision with me? On my desk sits a letter. It is from a nursing home and it reads as follows:

Dear Reverend:

Once again I am writing to all the ministers in the area, seeking their cooperation in taking services on Sunday afternoons at our local nursing home. These programs are held at 2:00 P.M. We would be grateful if you would aid us in this most important work.

Cordially,

Activities Superintendent

Should I do it, or should I not? As I debate the possibilities, memories flood my consciousness. One of them concerns feelings expressed to me long ago on a cold Monday morning by a disgusted Protestant minister.

"Never again will I take a service in that nursing home. The entire place simply regards me as an unpaid member of the staff whose chief task on Sunday afternoon is to provide worship and entertainment. Yesterday I had to set up my own chapel, dust off the furniture, and then round up the residents!"

Another recollection features an elderly nurse of great Christian charity who once ran a nursing home in the town of Cranberry Portage, Michigan. When she telephoned me for the fifth week in a row, asking me to conduct a Sunday afternoon service, I began to demur. In tears she explained:

"Reverend, I cannot get anybody else. And religious services are so important to our life here. And the patients are so hopeful that somebody will come!"

So, of course, I went . . .

Nobody denies that religious faith can be a strong bulwark in time of trouble, and in nursing homes all of God's children have troubles. Many residents suffer from severe mental and physical handicaps. Even when they are able to walk, hear, and see, they are surrounded by those who cannot. Visitors to these types of institutions often describe them as depressing or unfortunate. Despite the attempts by hard working staffs (and I have known many dedicated people who have worked in these places), nursing homes are full of lonely individuals who feel that there is nothing left for them in life . . . but death. Prayer has a habit of becoming very close to these people. Not infrequently, individuals who have ignored religion for seventy years or more will find themselves praying to God for pain to cease or sleep to come. Added to all this may be deep-set fears about finances or children from whom one never hears. How can one bring a service of public worship to bear on these things?

In many ways the attitude of pastor, staff, and patients is the key to the entire situation. Before any clergyman agrees to conduct worship in a nursing home, he should make sure that he has talked the situation over with administrators and, if possible, some of the patients. All

69

parties should understand the purposes of these services and the conditions under which they are to be held. Nobody can expect the atmosphere to duplicate the stained-glass aura of the pastor's local church, but that is not the same thing as saying that there should be no worship atmosphere at all.

The priest or minister who walks in three minutes before he is scheduled to begin and walks out just as fast when the service is over should not volunteer for this type of ministry. Likewise, the staff of a nursing home should not want a Sunday afternoon gathering just because every other nursing home in the area is having one. Everybody must understand that worship is an important piece of business and act accordingly. Here is an excellent chance to bring a liturgy into action that can do much to relieve emotional problems and even (as I have experienced privately) relieve physical distress. So there must be deliberate aims.

What could these possibly be? Healing is certainly one. Praying for love and cooperation between the residents could be another. Hope for eternal life might be a third. The list can readily expand with a little thought. Perhaps the use of oil as prescribed in the Epistle of James could become part of your approach. Almost always, residents of nursing homes appreciate your efforts if they can see that your worship is designed to help them. Seldom have I ever heard anybody object to my ministrations despite the fact that I have never conducted worship services in any nursing home where the congregation did not consist of many different denominations. But coupled with the aim should be the right atmosphere.

Psychology is supremely important in the praise of God; symbols, color, and light can go far to create the mood that at this time and in this place everybody present is engaged in the worship of God. A few flowers can take away drabness. A small table can serve as an altar. If possible, cover it with a clean white cloth. A cross of reasonable size, flanked by a pair of candlesticks, will help immensely. To one side should be a lectern so that the reader can see the print of the Bible without straining. A good adjunct is a collection plate.

The person in charge should wear the same vestments or robe that he or she wears in the parish church. Almost always there will be piano and hymnbooks, both of which can be very helpful. Although I have often led hymns with my voice, a musical instrument for singing is what most residents are used to. That means that an accompanist must be found. Where will you find such a person? It might seem easier to bring your own (and that may be necessary) but, if at all possible, use some person in the home.

Patients in nursing homes frequently have poor images of themselves and so almost always will defer to an outsider who is younger. An outside choir or organist can give a change of pace to your regular service, but do not use nonresidents too often! Private inquiries may disclose several patients who are willing, or even anxious, to work as ushers, Bible readers, and even acolytes. For these tasks I will train either men or women, and I have found that denominational background will often mean little. Even for those who cannot or will not be active, there should be opportunity to recite familiar prayers and sing well-known hymns. A responsive reading, such as a psalm, is also a good idea for those who can see well enough to read.

A theme has been selected, an atmosphere has been created, and people have been recruited to take part in the service. Now it remains to arrange the order for the liturgy.

It is wise to arrive early and watch carefully as your usher and the nursing home staff seat the residents. In a pinch you may have to do all this yourself. Place those with hearing and sight impairments in front; seat those who are likely to do distracting things in the rear. When all is quiet, have one of the residents light the candles if fire regulations will allow it. This acts as a signal that worship is about to begin. After the ushers have distributed the hymnbooks and opened them to the right page, announce your hymn.

After that opening, it might be wise to preach your sermon. There are two reasons for this. One, it gives you a chance to tell what the theme for today's worship is going to be; two, even the most handicapped of all your residents will still be alert. Then after a brief prayer, such as the Lord's Prayer, and a Bible reading, you can move toward the ceremony of anointing the sick. For this ancient rite use olive oil. When this service is done, whether publicly or privately, it should be kept short and simple. Carry the vial of oil in the left hand (unless you are lefthanded), and use the right thumb to do the anointing. Use a short prayer while you are placing the oil. Generally, I prefer a short statement that is easy to memorize and goes as follows: "I anoint you with oil, asking the mercy of our Lord Jesus Christ to remove all your pain and sickness. Amen."

If this ritual is not practical, then you can substitute intercessions, asking God to relieve the illness of those present. In my ministry, I encourage patients to tell me privately why they want these prayers; then I specifically mention the name of the resident and what he or she is requesting. It is wise to keep this type of prayer short.

After all is finished, a responsive reading around the theme of thanksgiving can be used—Psalm 133 is a possibility—or perhaps you may prefer a pastoral prayer. Then may follow another hymn during which the collection can be taken. The service should conclude by committing your congregation to God's care. And please, before your departure, visit with as many of the residents as you can!

Worship leaders can vary this order to suit the time and occasion. It is far more important to be loving and patient. Expect to be interrupted by residents whose mental abilities have been impaired. Do not be surprised if people get up and leave or arrive late. Many times you will have to wait while right hymn numbers are found by your helpers. In all probability, these disturbing things will distract the pastor more than the residents.

As the costs of nursing care reaches astronomical levels in our cities, the small-town pastor can expect more and more nursing homes placed in more and more small towns. Consequently, the amount of time he can spend on this ministry can do nothing but increase. Coupled with this will be the very necessary and important task of keeping relatives informed about the physical and mental state of the patients.

The burden could become overwhelming.

On my desk sits a letter. It is from a nursing home and it reads as follows.

Dear Reverend:

Once again I am writing to all the ministers in the area, seeking their cooperation in taking services on Sunday afternoons at our local nursing home. These programs are held at 2:00 P.M. We would be grateful if you would aid us in this most important event.

Cordially,

Activities Superintendent

Shall I do it? Yes, of course I shall. And Paul, I hope that in your ministry at Bypass you will always be willing to aid your local nursing home.

Cordially,

A. M. Upchurch, Dean

# IX

# Christian Charm? Whatever Next!

"Nuts! Go as you are."

"I can't do it."

"Why not? I would."

Then he said a wise and memorable thing. "You got to be awful rich to dress as bad as you do," he said. (John Steinbeck—*Travels with Charley*)

The Girl in Red Motel
Cranberry Portage, Michigan

Dear Pastor Stanbury,

Tell me, Reverend Sir, am I allowed to wonder at funerals? Especially at the funeral of an aunt? And further—am I allowed to make the object of my speculation the dress of the officiating pastor? Please, Sir—a retort!

All of these questions arose yesterday evening when I was sitting in the Cranberry Portage Funeral Home, going through the small-town ritual of accepting condolences on the death of my aunt. Since she was nearly a hundred years of age and had outlived most of her friends and all of her brothers and sisters, the family had selected me to preside. Being an old hand at this sort of thing, my first action was to select a base of operations, which in this case happened to be a chair standing behind and slightly to the left of a large wreath of flowers. About 8:30 P.M. I was reduced to sitting in my place of refuge and looking over and under the blossoms and examining the rug. I had just made the delightful discovery that the special arrow design in the carpet was artfully woven to carry one's eye from any part of the room directly toward the casket when my research was suddenly interrupted by a pair of fire-engine red sneakers enclosing a pair of bright orange socks. Startled, I began to raise my head and then saw that the orange socks gave way to a pair of faded blue jeans that rose in long straight lines until they in turn yielded to the brightest yellow shirt I had seen in years. Of course, I blinked—twice. When my eyes were again in focus, I became aware of a streaky white clerical collar which materialized from the upper reaches of the shirt, covered the general vicinity of the Adam's apple and then retreated into the confines of some looped cloth. In turn, this band was partially concealed by long golden hair that drooped in uncut splendor over a pair of thin shoulders. My heart skipped a beat! Could this be the blond beast, beloved of Nietzsche, come to carry off a seventy-year-old lady to his lair? Was it a golden-haired Greek in search of Helen? Alas for my literary imagination! Our blond gentleman, clad in such resplendent raiment of red, orange, gold, and white was only the Reverend hired by the Cranberry Portage mortician to bury my relative. What a disappointment for an elderly romantic woman!

Yet, in the loneliness of my hotel room, I am puzzled. Why have I run into this subject of clerical dress at least three times in the past week? First, there was your sermon of last Sunday—you know, the one about "the lilies of the field." Then there were Joy Jones's remarks at the women's meeting on Tuesday, which dealt long and lovingly on your general sloppy appearance. And now     the blond pastor! Has God appointed me to become an instrument for reforming clerical dress? I agree that in some instances a great deal of reform is needed, but why pick on an old school teacher? Surely, there are others who are better qualified. And yet the inclination is there! My love is Saint Stephen's Parish, and I do not want its reputation diminished; but I am afraid that your messy appearance of late is doing just that. As for Joy—well, she is a pain when she begins to criticize you; and I would like you to remove the cause of her dislike. Finally, I have always been known as a smart dresser; and so I suppose there is a bit of vanity mixed up in all of this somewhere . . . together with some pain, for I do not like to see any parson—especially one from my own parish—make obvious mistakes. And the mistake includes not only your general appearance but also that sermon you preached last Sunday. Arguing that Jesus' injunction about the lilies of the field means that no Christian should be concerned about the way he dresses is such a stupid premise that my dander is really up! Did you prepare that talk beforehand, or did you steal it from the broadcast of Carl Marshall over radio station WAVE? It comes on at 9:00 P.M. Saturdays, and you and he certainly had the same slant on that passage from Matthew. Let me refresh your memory by looking up the verses. They are from the sixth chapter of that Gospel.

And why take ye thought for raiment? Consider the lilies of the field, how they grow; they toil not, neither do they spin: And yet I say unto you, That even Solomon in all his glory was not arrayed like one of these. Wherefore, if God so clothe the grass of the field, which today is, and to morrow is cast into the oven, shall he not much more clothe you, O ye of little faith?

Truthfully, you and Carl Marshall are not the only preachers who have argued that these verses are meant to strike down vanity of dress—but I must be pardoned if I disagree! Jesus is not saying that one ought not to be properly dressed—indeed his metaphor about the beauty of the flowers could give quite the opposite impression. The emphasis is on worry; the real meaning of "take ye thought" is "Why are you full of care?" The idea is clear enough in English—if you examine the entire passage. Now, it is true that at one time certain Christians cultivated body lice and ragged costumes, believing them to be a mark of sainthood. Around Bypass, however, we take a slightly different view of the matter—especially if your name is Joy Jones.

Of course, Joy is a professional clergy-hater—something I admit, even if I am fond of her company. You will find members of this long-nosed species scattered among the parishes of any small town. Generally speaking, their tendencies toward pastor paranoia can best be dismissed by quiet silence—but Joy is different. She has an instinct for the truth that transcends her emotions, and her shrillness and intensity give her a following at Saint Stephen's that cannot be ignored. Last Tuesday, she took over the women's meeting and spent long and laborious moments over your unshaved looks, your uncut hair, and general sloppy appearance. Since she was right, there was little that I could do, except to warn you that objections are being raised in the parish about your looks. Encountering in the course of a single week a clergyman who comes to bury my aunt, and in the process tries too hard with his dress, and another who, not only does not try to look right, but defends his attitude in a sermon is a bit more than one my age cares to take!

All right, pastor—I have displayed my motivations! You might say that, literally, I am objecting to the cloth! Therefore, having hit at what may be a sensitive spot, allow me to expand my domain a little farther and take on a banker. More specifically, good old, tightfisted Arthur J. Fillmore, the president of Bypass State.

Now, I am sure that you have seen Arthur J. sitting in his office all dressed up in his black Brooks Brothers suit, looking as if he would like to foreclose on every piggy bank in town. Believe it or not, there is another side to Arthur J.; but to see it you will have to attend the annual Mother's Day picnic that Bypass State Bank sponsors in the town park. Arthur J. founded this event in honor of his mother and spares neither money nor effort in making it a huge success. On this occasion his Brooks Brothers suit is laid aside in order that he may don an ancient apron that has plastered across its front such sentiments as Ye Old Cook and Bottle Washer and Don't Laugh Lady; I Just Gave Your Boyfriend an Ulcer. I am sure that Arthur J. would not exchange that garment for a thousand-dollar United States Treasury bill; for, as soon as he puts it on, he becomes a different individual—much like the boy hero who discovered the school in flames. Everybody present is his friend; nobody else is allowed to pour gallons of sauce over the roasting chickens. Arthur J. in his Brooks Brothers suit and Arthur J. in his apron are two distinct persons. If asked, I am sure that everyone in Bypass would say that socially they prefer Arthur J. the cook to Arthur J. the banker, but that comment is too simple. Life in Bypass centers much more around banks than around picnics; most of us would not take Arthur J. very seriously if he doled out money in his cook's apron. Likewise, nobody is likely to take ill-dressed parsons seriously.

Clothes hide nakedness, keep you warm—and attract attention. In a very real way they advertise our functions in life and how we view ourselves. They can work for you or against you; they can help a small-town parson create the correct impression, or they can give you an aura that no professional individual would ever desire. Consequently, it behooves every small-town pastor to consider his appearance carefully in terms of his profession and in terms of his self-image. To this I would add a third criterion—the most important of all. He should know the way his parishioners see him. This latter point is worth a bit of expansion.

To begin, parishioners have a tendency to place their pastor on a certain social level. This plateau may differ from individual to individual, but it is a good rule of thumb to say that the social grade you are assigned will be no lower than the one your parishioner accepts as his own. A clergyperson's standard of dress should not be lower than the one your parishioners have adopted, for nobody appreciates a type of apparel that ranks less than that. My Aunt Hattie—the same one that is being buried today—was very conscious of a small town's makeup and sometimes recited a piece of doggerel to illustrate this idea.

> Birds of a feather,
> Flock together.
> To keep us ever
> From going nether!

In small towns this is a simple fact. Let a neighbor ignore the paint on his buildings, and those who live close will criticize; let a person dress below the standards of his associates, and everybody notices and begins to feel uncomfortable. As for our clergy, we like a pastor who dresses as well as we do. It is a serious error, believe me, for a parson to seek deliberately a style of appearance that clashes with the ones his parishioners think are decent. Unfortunately, as far as pastors are concerned, that measure may be higher than they like.

The clue to all this is the way people in small towns dress for worship. Now, I understand that there are parishes where casual apparel is accepted at all church functions; but, as the actions of Joy have just illustrated, this is not true at Saint Stephen's. Of course most parishioners, if asked, will tell you that they do not care what the neighbor wears to church. That will not be the only time they say one thing and do the opposite! Always, Mr. and Mrs. Average Parishioner will have one suit of clothes or one dress carefully preserved for higher social occasions, and church-going in rural communities is always considered a higher social occasion.

The reasons for this may be difficult to analyze. Just take my word for it!

I mention these things because the last three pastors appointed to Saint Stephen's have done their level best to appear at all times friendly and approachable. This disposition was, of course, deliberate; and consequently the role became forced. In part, each of the three made his clothes fit his style whenever possible; and church meetings and house calls were not excepted. Certainly, we appreciated what each one was trying to do—I emphasize the word "trying"—but in the process two of the three ceased to be effective clergy. Saint Paul advised us to become all things to all men, but he neglected to add that it is difficult to do without compromising Christian ethics. Naturally, parishioners want an easy, relaxed atmosphere; and clothes can help create that mood. Again, I have run into the argument that strangers will be frightened by too much formal clothing at a church service; and, therefore, a well-dressed pastor will advertise himself as basically uncongenial and hard to meet. No doubt, clergy have a heavy role to play in small towns, and not the least difficult part of that role is the formidable business of keeping their professional standards intact without alienating their congregation. In a sense you are required to balance two levels of existence; but, if you are going to err, it is best to err on the side of your professional standards and not on the side of "becoming one of the boys." Still, I have a hard time understanding why a well-dressed man cannot instill a feeling of friendship and warmth into the conversation. A smile, an amiable remark, an easy handshake can come as easily from one who is neatly attired as from one who is not. Why should a properly clothed parson cease to be human?

Complementary to this is the position that communities expect their clergy to hold and to act. All the townsfolk, whether they belong to your parish or not, will want to know you. This means that it is best if you are highly visible, and one of the best ways to be highly visible is to dress well. Leaders in small towns are frequently past masters at remaining hidden, but that grace cannot be granted to you. When a parishioner is listening to a sermon, he would like it to come from a pastor who looks like a parson.

That thought has led me back to my aunt's funeral and to the real reason I shall find our multicolored Cranberry Portage Reverend difficult to accept. It is not so much his clothes that are upsetting; it is the message these clothes bring. Of course, I understand what he wants to accomplish; his dress screams the message that he wishes to relate to the young people of his parish and community. But . . . what about those who are not young? At this afternoon's service, everybody—including the corpse—will be older than the preacher. All during that period our officiant's attire will say, "Behold! I am not interested in you."

If two former rectors of Saint Stephen's erred by becoming so informal that they ceased to be full clergymen, our Cranberry Portage parson has erred by saying that he wishes to minister to only part of his constituency. If I felt that he was just being himself—that this way of dress was natural—I could be more tolerant; but, after meeting him last evening, I am sure that the red sneakers, the blue jeans, and the uncut hair-do come, not from a desire to be individualistic, but from a wish to conform to the youth cult of America. In no way was his apparel informal or unplanned; in its own way, it was as smart and ostentatious as a black tie and tails. Now comes the important question. Will this approach work in a small congregation?

No doubt there are times and places for this type of attire, but that time and place is not in Bypass or Cranberry Portage. My reasoning is simple enough—look at the parish register of Saint Stephen's, and you will see the drift of my thought. Like most small town congregations, your parish does not represent the age distribution of America; the bulk of your congregation are either children, middle-aged, or elderly. Your records will disclose that a high percentage of your adult parishioners were confirmed in their forties and fifties. Added to this is the fact that many of your grownups who were confirmed as children, left the parish in their early youth, and did not return until their children were ready for confirmation. Thus, a pastor who wishes to make his appearance conform to the standards of youth must be warned that he is favoring the least populous part of his parish. This pattern seems true for most of rural America; it is the middle-aged who seem the most ripe for evangelism, not the youth. Therefore, if our Cranberry Portage Reverend wanted to identify with those most likely to be affected by the Christian gospel, he should have dressed as a mature adult.

Briefly, I pause at my own audacity. Pastor, I have committed heresy! In the midst of a discourse on clergy apparel, I have stated that one should purchase one's clothing with the middle-aged and elderly in mind! Before you dismiss all this as the ravings of an out-of-date lady parishioner, look around you. Despite all the organizations, rallies, and emphasis on young people, those in their salad days remain the least affected and impressed by the church. It is the middle-aged and elderly who, knowing what life can be, value the church's message that the world can be overcome.

I have wandered from the main point—the reasons why a man of the cloth should pay attention to his appearance in a small town. A possible biblical objection has been discussed; the atmosphere your appearance creates was illustrated by that frozen mackerel, Arthur J. Fillmore; the attitude of your parishioners toward attire and church-going was used as a guide to your own standard of dress; the contention that a well-dressed parson sets a barrier between himself and members of the community was dismissed, and the danger of letting your clothing always cater to just one section of your parish has been noted. We ought to be finished . . . except one other matter keeps nagging me and will not be still. Pastor Stanbury, I think the real reason why your appearance is sloppy can be summed up in one word—laziness!

Have I smashed our friendship forever? Can I proceed to the end of the missive without having it torn to shreds? I certainly hope so . . . for this composition has been a great deal of work and cost me much thought.

Laziness, I am told, is largely an emotional state related to one's view of one's self; and I well believe it. An individual whose self-esteem is low finds it difficult to dress well. In this vein, do not confuse expensive clothing with correct appearance. A rumpled three-piece suit mated with mismatched socks cannot compete with an inexpensive, but carefully selected, sports outfit. Cleanliness and neatness, coupled with a flair for what pleases the eye, count much more than high price. The trick lies in studying and knowing the art of appearing correctly. There are plenty of books and magazines that can teach you that, but far too often individuals with a poor self-image do not take the time and trouble to study the art of dressing. They should!

Good clothing can improve your feelings about yourself, heighten confidence, and declare war on the low periods of life.

I am becoming maudlin! Enough of my advice; it is time for me to go to lunch and prepare for this afternoon's service. You need—and I need—another slant on my argument. What could be better than a Methodist one—especially if it came from the founder himself?

The author of a book I secured yesterday afternoon from the Cranberry Portage Library claimed that the founder of the Methodist Church was a "neat preacher." To our ears that implies that he had the ear of the young—but let John Wesley express his own feelings on the subject:

Let it be observed, that slovenliness is no part of religion; that neither this nor any text of scripture condemns neatness of apparel. Certainly this is a duty not a sin. Cleanliness is, indeed, next to godliness.

Your loving friend,
Mary Walsh

# X

# Say, People—
# Do I Have to Get Up in the Morning?

He only earns his freedom and existence, who daily conquers
them. (Goethe)

Jubilee Seminary
Collegetown, U.S.A.

Dear Paul,

Tea . . . cookies . . . conversation. Especially conversation! All during Holy Week and Easter, I have been
considering your recent visit to Jubilee and that hour you
spent talking to me. As for that discourse . . . let it wait a bit
until I clear my own conscience.

Paul, I have no desire to intrude into your private
emotions! Well—I guess that strictly speaking that is not
true, but my language shows the indecision I am feeling
toward what I am about to say. I can only plead friendship
as the cause of both my writing and my hesitation.
Certainly, I have no wish to lose your good will and esteem,
but on the other hand I have no desire to see you remain in
your desperate "down mood." Now, as you will shortly
see, my personal history gives a partial explanation for my
writing; but there is more to this tome than subjective
experience. Clerical depression is one of the most common
things affecting parsons and one of the most common
things that parsons never discuss. In a way it belongs to the

85

shadows of our profession—to a world that pastors often help others to traverse, but one in which they would never admit to dwelling personally. Pastors are always supposed to "live with the Lord"—how American Christians take that for granted!—and that notion is subtly reinforced week after week by many a television and radio preacher. Paul, the truth is far different! The kingdom of Heaven is a difficult objective to obtain, and one of the chief obstacles many need to overcome is their tendency toward melancholy. Ever has it seemed to be thus! If seventeenth-century English Congregationalism can be said to have produced a spiritual soul, I am certain that most would have to vote for John Bunyan—and yet read how he described himself while in the grip of a severe religious depression:

By reason of that [Bunyan's sense of sin] I was more loathsome in my own eyes than was a toad; and I thought I was so in God's eyes too. Sin and corruption, I said, would as naturally bubble out of my heart as water out of a fountain. I could have changed heart with anybody. I thought none but the Devil himself could equal me for inward wickedness and pollution of mind. Sure thought I, I am forsaken of God; and thus I continued a long while, even for some years together.

What a state! Who would possibly be attracted to it? Yet, even now, melancholy has a fascination for the intellectual mind; there is an attractive side to it. Do you recall Auden's poem "The Age of Anxiety"? Its impact has been so great that it has inspired both a symphony and a ballet. Let us not forget that more than one pastor has been known to rationalize his thinking in terms of popular fashion. Is it possible that you have this inclination? Recall our conversation at Jubilee and judge for yourself.

Me: You are very quiet today, Paul. That's not like you!

Paul: Oh, I just decided to get away from Saint Stephen's for a few days.

Me: In Holy Week!

Paul: Well, it is only Tuesday in Holy Week. Anyway, my congregation will not really care where I am or what I do. You should have seen our Palm Sunday attendance.

Me: Low, eh? How does it compare to last year's?

Paul: I don't know. Didn't bother to look it up. But take my word for it, it was poor.

Me: Have some tea and a cookie. The cookies are really quite good—chocolate and nuts blended together. Might cheer you up.

Paul: I don't want to be cheered up. No thanks, I'll skip the cookie. I am not very hungry when I get in one of these moods. To tell the unvarnished truth, I am just plain fed up with Bypass and Saint Stephen's. You know—they did not even make a good Every Member Canvass this year.

Me: You are sure you won't have a cookie? They are very good. As far as your canvass is concerned, Dean Upchurch tells me that Saint Stephen's had not bothered with one for years. So anything you did would have been an improvement.

Paul: That's the whole trouble in a nutshell! They haven't done anything in that place for years and have every intention of improving on that record! I don't understand them, and they don't understand me. The entire church makes me feel as if I had a large weight on my stomach.

Me: You mean that you are depressed about your job?

Paul: You can say that in spades! And when I consulted with my clerical brethren in Bypass on this, do you know what the Christian minister said? "Welcome to the club!"

87

And so on . . . and on . . . and on.

Believe me, I know how you felt and perhaps still do, for I can bear witness to the fact that this malady often struck me when I was a parish clergyman. Through study, a rather peculiar happening, and a determination to shake this type of mood, I finally outgrew it; but . . . oh, my friend, I know its terrors well—as do several of my clerical friends. For hours I have listened to their notions that they are locked into an intolerable position with which they cannot cope and from which they cannot escape. Even writers of the Old Testament have known the terrors of the blues—remember King Saul and Job?—but it has never been better expressed than by the writer of Psalm 22.

> I am poured out like water
> all my bones are loosened.
> My heart within my breast is melting wax.
> My strength is dried out like a pot-sherd;
> my tongue sticks to the roof of my mouth
> and you have laid me in the dust of the grave!

One of the interesting phenomena that preceded these attacks in my case—and I do not hesitate to call them just that—was a gigantic feeling of turbulence within. Giant fires were raging; my feelings were deep and strong, but almost always they were negative in tenor. Despite all my training, I found it difficult to express my anger and frustration; for, after all, clergy are supposed to be kind and benign individuals. These raging moods would be succeeded by ones in which I was filled with almost complete inertia; I would feel that all my sermons, all my work as a counselor, and all my expensive education had been and were being wasted. Rationally, I knew that it was not so; for there was more than one marriage within my parish that was still functioning because of my skill and, besides, building campaigns do take talent! Reason, however, had little to do with my feelings; for suspicion filled my being. Mistrust of my fellowmen and of myself soon led to mistrust of my religion; the great doctrines of the church were weighed in the balance and found wanting. I felt that the Lord did not even know that I existed. What had he done for me lately?

It is not necessary for me to recite any more of my past history: I do it only to show the depths to which this type of mood can go. What is of more importance are the steps that I took to break myself out of the habit—for blue moods are habits—and how my experiences can be profitable to you. The climax of my deliverance came by way of a dream— believe it or not—but that was not the first step, or even the second. For those who wish to be free of this strong master must first resolve that it will not conquer them, but that they will be the victors. What I am discussing here is an absolute act of the will, taken with the firm intent that the victim will do everything in his power to break loose from the domination of this pattern. To a Christian, of course, that means enrolling God as your partner; but I am convinced that, in the majority of cases, God will not help without the petitioner's active cooperation.

The best parallel I can draw at this early stage of deliverance is one between depression and alcoholism. There are scores of people who like being drunk just as there are scores of people who like being sad. How this possibly can be is hard to understand; but, believe me, the attraction does exist. English intellectuals knew this well.

> When I go musing all alone
> Thinking of divers things foreknown;
> When I build castles in the air,
> Void of sorrow and void of fear,
> Pleasing myself with phantasms sweet,
> Methinks the time runs very fleet.
> > All my joys to this are folly;
> > Naught so sweet as melancholy.

There was a side to Robert Burton that loved sadness; this was one of the first things I noticed in myself. It was my actions—especially my terse speech and my slow wearying movements that convinced me that the underlying mood that lay beneath them must be destroyed. But how . . . and when . . . I could not have told you.

Being the type of person that I am and having once resolved to rid myself of the malady, I consulted another clergyman. He advised me to read everything I could about the subject, and when I grew tired of that exercise to just go on reading. Thus one afternoon, in a less pensive mood than usual, I picked up an old edition of Chaucer and turned to the "Parson's Tale." It was quite a surprise to learn that the old boy knew something about the disease, and even more of a surprise to discover that he knew Saint Paul had discussed it with the Corinthians.

"Then comes the sin of worldly sorrow, such as is called 'Tristica' [the blues]," says Chaucer, "that slays man as says Saint Paul."

What could the writers of the Middle Ages know about depression? What possible value was there in Saint Paul? Didn't both ascribe mental problems to devils and unclean spirits? Well . . . not all the time! The passage Chaucer had in mind was from Second Corinthians, but most intriguing was the way theologians between the time of Paul and Chaucer had interpreted it. Paul had divided sorrow into two parts—godly and worldly—and some Christian writers had built on that notion to see depression as divided into two parts. There was the rational type—the one whose causes you could understand—and the irrational sort—the ones whose origins were unknown. Or were they?

Learned people of the medieval period claimed the cause of depression lay in sin, but I could not grant their arguments. So I left them and went instead to modern psychology, and especially to Freud. Now, Paul, despite the joy of my discovery, I cannot argue that it will be the correct explanation for all people at all times; I can only put it forth as the clue that enabled me to understand my condition. Modern writers on this subject tell me that depression is best understood as a broad mosaic that includes biochemical factors, childhood experiences, stress, and possible heredity. To me, however, these interpretations were unsatisfactory; for, if you granted their exclusiveness, you would also have to grant that nobody could prevent or control the causes of down-patterns. My disposition, my training, and, above all, my Christianity found such a conclusion intolerable; therefore, I turned, as I have said, to Freud—the one man who would have told me that my religious motivations were fantasy!

One evening, while pursuing Freud's Ego and Id, I found my mind wandering. Therefore, I turned off the light and fell into a drowsy state. Into my tired mind came a figure clothed in dark blue, tightly muffled, and holding in his hand a candy box. In no way did the figure appear sinister; he was tall, well built, and nicely groomed—rather like some person getting ready to go off to a masked ball. Slowly he approached and showed me the box in his hand. Beneath and just to the right of a large ribbon—the view was very sharp and very clear—were inscribed in large black letters—"The Sweets of Self-Love." I shook myself awake and wrote down the dream before it was forgotten. Yet I knew, even as I wrote, that I had discovered the reason for my mood. The gentleman was, of course, myself. He was disguised because I would not admit my shortcoming, and the candy was how I pictured my ability.

Now, I can smile at the idea that my talents were not being used properly, but in those days I did not smile—I raged! Remember how I described some moments of anger as preceding these attacks of depression? One would assume that they were totally different, but close observation and thought will disclose that they do have one link. Each had

91

"me" as the central object of affection. Well was that box labeled "The Sweets of Self-Love!"

Does my analysis seem farfetched? Can we count on one solitary incident to give so much truth—even if its Freudian connection is so clear as to need no further explanation? Should you feel this way, take a few moments with me and listen to Antonio, a Shakespearean character who first saw the light of day in *The Merchant of Venice*, discuss his blue period.

> In sooth I know not why I am so sad.
> It wearies me: you say it wearies you.
> But how I caught it, found it, or came by it
> What stuff 'tis made of, whereof it is born,
> I am to learn;
> And such a want-wit, sadness makes of me
> That I have much ado to know myself.

Antonio would have been well advised to write out his speech and then count the number of times he uses "I," "me," and "myself." But . . . why should the advice be limited to Antonio? I always feel that it is well for every pastor who has a tendency to become depressed—even if it is for short periods—to keep a journal. All of us who know down-periods also know a divided will and a lack of explosive intensity that encourages us to seek outlets for the internal storms that cause so much grief and trouble.

Yet, external outlets there must be! How important I feel they are for pastors who are prone to the blues! Clergy who are subject to sadness are often given to introspection and brooding. Frankly, it is well for parsons of this type to look for clerical friends who are normal, but nonreflective; ones who put more emphasis on action than on thought. Of course, there is much about "action parsons" that is difficult for a "reflective parson" to appreciate; not infrequently the former type gets his parish and himself into trouble because he acts on impulse and not on reason. This is likely to disturb a "reflective parson"! Despite this, I have always found impetuous people a good antidote for my own style.

More important is the necessity to become committed and involved in something that cannot aid you directly. It is not an accident that I am a member of the local library board. Interested in books and civic duties I am, but I am also interested in my mental health. The library enables me to concentrate on something that I enjoy, but in no way will it aid either my fortune or my career. Indeed, it might do exactly the opposite! What it does is to allow me to get away from the church, the college, and the students and devote my time to something in whose success or failure I have no personal stake—except for the fact that it enables me to fight my self-centeredness. To this I would add the admonition that those clergy subject to depression must learn to be kind to themselves. Not infrequently, we who are disposed to melancholia find it easier to give to others than to ourselves.

Too much of this epistle has been autobiographical in tone, and I have no wish to appear expert on such a complex subject. Yet I cannot leave off without saying something about one of the most devastating drawbacks of clerical depression—the way it can leave your faith in tatters. Consequently, let me solve my dilemma by going back to Bunyan. I spoke of his religious depression; now let us speak of religious deliverance—or at least the beginnings of it. Bunyan had begun to read the Bible, searching for appropriate texts and found:

This made a strange seizure on my spirit; it brought light with it and commanded a silence in my heart of all those tumultuous thoughts that before did use, like masterless hellhounds, to roar and bellow and make a hideous noise within me. It showed me that Jesus Christ had not quite forsaken and cast off my Soul.

By chance I came across this passage one day, and it caused me to give up my search for answers to my malady among the classical theologians and psychologists—as useful as they had been—and to concentrate on Bunyan's plan. My method was to begin saying the Episcopal service of Morning Prayer again, but this time to pay strict attention to the psalms and scripture readings as they came up in regular rotation. What I was after were verses or groups of verses that would remind me of God's grace, love, or providence. It was interesting how often I found them! In this search I was not concerned with great doctrinal proofs or with the length of time I might be sustained; the idea of God's love was enough to get me through a few hours, and then it was time to read the passage again. In this way my faith was restored.

Although I firmly believe that there can be no faith without doubt, I am convinced that it is a waste of time to meet those doubts by intellectual arguments when one is gripped by depression. No pastor can think his way into salvation; there is too much theology reminding us that man is not entirely good. On the other hand, there is a lot of theology that says that he is not entirely bad—a point I wish more sermons would make. A pastor confronted with a shrinking faith needs kindness, the company of other clergy who have gone through the same crisis and survived with enhanced confidence, and the realization that the Christian life does not spring into being fully equipped and perfect in all details. In many ways the religious life of every Christian is a pilgrimage and a contest against natural inclinations— and to many a feeling of the blues is a natural habit. When living through a down-period, work and live as a child!

Small churches and small towns have their own patterns and ways of considering things. Often, sensitive clergy who are stationed within them find these weighing heavily on their souls. So . . . get out of town at least once a week! Visit other pastors and other parishes; it will help keep things in perspective. Go to concerts and art exhibits; it will give your cultural impulses a chance to be fulfilled. Find a girlfriend; she will get your mind off yourself and your troubles!

Clergy—especially those is small towns—need to turn their talents into directions that will give them a sense of accomplishment, and they should not be afraid to look outside their own church in order to discover at least a part of it. Diocesan officials could help, if they were aware of the problem and were willing to give pastors in small parishes more recognition; but don't expect that to happen! Work out your own salvation as far as your feelings are concerned, and I hope that the example of one who has traveled that road and learned how to cope—at least in part—will turn out to be useful.

In truth, I am strongly tempted not to mail this letter, for it tells much about myself. Again, it may threaten our friendship. On the other hand, if friendship is worth anything, it is worth risking experience and sensitivity.

With all good wishes,
Theophilus Ignatius, Principal
Jubilee Seminary

# XI

# Women at the Altar?
# Over My Dead Body!

You can always tell a conservative churchman, but you cannot tell him much. (Old Episcopal Saying)

Canterbury Street<br>Palestine, Michigan

Dear Paul,

This morning's mail brought some interesting correspondence. There was an advertisement from a California vineyard—buy our communion wine by the barrel. Then came a note from the bishop's office stating that this year's mite-box offering will be sent to Saint Ephrem of Edessa Girls' School, Egbado, Nigeria, "and would we please be prompt with the remittance?" Finally there was a short but burning epistle from a Mrs. Katherine K. Kaltenborne of your parish. Of the three pieces of mail, Mrs. Kaltenborne's is by far the most interesting. She begins by reminding me that she has been a faithful parishioner of Saint Stephen's for many years and has known me for an equal length of time. She continues by saying that it is with great reluctance that she has been forced to write, but, when a young clergyman (meaning you) departs from ancient liturgical custom, she feels compelled to draw it to the attention of the proper authority (meaning me). Her consternation arose from your service of worship last Sunday. Mrs. Kaltenborne showed up late and was pleased to see that for the first time in several years Saint Stephen's had acquired an acolyte. Her joy, however, was short-lived; imagine her consternation when the book was moved for the reading of the Gospel and the altar boy turned out to be a girl! "Such new actions," she states, "are very disturbing to those who love the church. Women's Liberation does not belong around the altar!" She ends the letter by stating that she has "no wish to make an open issue of this matter within the parish and therefore trusts that I will deal with the innovation speedily."

Ordinarily, I would dismiss the matter with a polite note. Whatever I may think of girl acolytes, you are certainly within your rights to use them—especially since there is an obvious reluctance on the part of the parish males to step into the breach. Reflection tells me, however, that this is not an ordinary situation. I know Mrs. Kaltenborne quite well and the devotion she has had for many years toward Saint Stephen's. Again, she is not without influence in the community, and that means she has credit in the church. Faithful old parish families are always a force, and Mrs. K. K. K. fits that description quite well. Finally, she belongs to a wing in this denomination that has been hurt mightily by change, and hurt people need the church's love. Parishioners like Katherine are well worth examining.

The sketch need not be extensive; genuine conservatives are quite free with their views. They dislike change and have a horror of chaos. To these people the church meets their needs just as it is, and they can see no reason to encourage its venture into unchartered waters. The most important words in the English language for understanding conservative church people are "security" and "order." If you wish to win them over to your side your first task is to see that neither of these conditions is in danger. Gentleness and understanding are the best tools in your arsenal; arguments, confrontations, and loud scenes are to be avoided as much as possible. Above everything else, do not get into controversies centering around church traditions or biblical proof texts. You can prove everything and anything you like by delving into the recesses of church history or by looking for scriptural passages that demonstrate positions you have previously selected. Now, I have nothing against church tradition and even less bias against the Bible, but—this is a game that two can play. For example, suppose you go to Saint Paul looking for a passage that would demonstrate his approval of lady acolytes. In Galatians you would discover that he said, "In Christ there is neither male nor female." Doubtless, Katherine, being a good church person, would also consult the saint. She would ignore Galatians, for it would not suit her purposes; but the Pastoral Epistles—especially the ones to Timothy—would prove more profitable. The advice "suffer not a woman to usurp" should do quite nicely as far as Mrs. K. K. K. is concerned. If Saint Paul had been a little more thoughtful and given us clear-cut instructions about girl acolytes, the argument could be settled by going to his writings; but unfortunately he never saw fit to do it. Anyway, in the final analysis, ultraconservative people do not change their positions because of the opposition's theological arguments. The reason is simple enough; they always think their doctrinal views represent the soundest interpretation possible.

Doubtless, by this time, Paul, you are finding both Katherine and me a bit wearying. Being fresh from seminary, you may think through your recent training that Mrs. K. K. K. is not exactly what she seems to be. I assure you that she is—I know her well enough to say that—but you would be amiss if you did not examine the credentials of most parish dissenters with care. Christians are members of churches for a good many reasons; and sometimes these reasons have nothing to do with truth, high ideals, or righteousness. Every clergyman worth his salt learns that lesson sooner or later—sometimes to his grief—but always to his enlightenment. Yet, in this situation I am convinced that the lady had and has no hidden motivations. Put in its simplest terms, she does not like girl acolytes and you find them acceptable. Now . . . is it possible for moves to be made before you two end up in your respective deep-freezes? I do not know, but the rest of the letter will take for granted that it is.

As a self-appointed referee on this situation, my first task is to examine more closely the attitudes of the people involved. Suppose I begin by asking myself how Katherine sees you. Doubtless, I would write such expressions as young, radical, and liturgical innovator. If I were to reverse the process and put down your opinion of Katherine, I would find such terms as conservative, old fogey, diehard, and difficult. Suppose I carry the game a bit further and wonder how each of you would grade his or her own attitudes. I would bet that now such words as discreet, restrained, moderate, and prudent would be used. This makes it very clear that you will never succeed in having Mrs. Kaltenborne see herself as you see her by direct confrontations. In other words—swallow your feelings, Paul, and think this thing through with care! Don't label Mrs. K. K. K. as your emotions are now dictating.

This brings us to a consideration of strategy. Perhaps you may just conclude that the whole problem is not worth a battle and give up. It is true that in many cases a wise clergyman is like the Duke of Wellington—he knows when to retreat—but in this instance I would not advise it. For all practical purposes this denomination has decided that girls can serve at the altar. I, as you well know, do not agree with the decision; but that is not the point. Like it or not, a single parish—or for that matter a single individual—cannot be considered wiser than the entire church, unless somebody or something has been granted a direct revelation from heaven; and not even Katherine is claiming that. Moreover, to exclude your girls from this duty is to hurt them, and too many good church people have been hurt by the conservative views of others. Most important of all, you cannot allow Katherine to win on this issue. Everybody at Saint Stephen's knows that behind Mrs. Kaltenborne's moves is a challenge to your legitimate authority. Frequently, it is not judicious for a pastor to exercise his rights; but in this case I do not think you can argue even that. Therefore your best course of action will be to try to reconcile Mrs. Kaltenborne to the inevitable. That may not be as difficult as it first appears.

If you move carefully, you are in a much stronger position than Katherine. I am on your side—despite my feelings about girl acolytes—and I am sure that the girls and their parents will like what you are doing. Again, hundreds of parishes have adopted the custom of using girls at the altar. You can argue, with a good deal of justification, that the parish forced you to take this step because the males of the Bypass church dodged the issue. Consequently, I believe offensive action is called for on this question . . . but remember that the word "offensive" has two meanings. We want movement, not annoyance. A working plan is needed and so . . . let me introduce you to the Ain't-Really-Black-Method.

The Ain't-Really-Black-Method is something I discovered quite by accident in my first parish at Cranberry Portage. Like your present difficulties, this also arose over a shortage of altar boys. Finally, one of our black members, the president of the women's association, prevailed upon her nephew Peter to volunteer as Saint Luke's one and only server. Of course, I was delighted to accept him; and within a few weeks he was fully trained and ready to serve his first Eucharist. On the preceding Wednesday, I went visiting, as was my custom, and ended up in the home of one of our elderly white male parishioners. In the course of the conversation, he informed me that he had moved to Cranberry Portage in order to get away from "them." In the

United States of the fifties, "them" could mean only one thing—American Blacks! You can imagine my feelings as I listened to his prattle, but by the grace of God—it could not have been my intelligence—I got out of there without a fight, went home, and worried for three solid days. Next Sunday the old gentleman showed up, talkative as ever, and proceeded to occupy the north side of the second pew on the left. Peter and his aunt also came into the church, and the aunt chose the south side of the same pew. Peter, happy in his new position, delivered the bread and wine on cue, moved the book on cue and tolled—at least that is the way it sounded to me—the Sanctus bell on cue. By the end of the service I was a nervous wreck, fleeing to the kitchen as soon as the blessing was pronounced and before the last hymn. Rather surprised, the congregation trailed after me. Quite at ease the black lady poured coffee for the elderly white gentleman and engaged him in a conversation about child-rearing. The rest of the congregation spent most of its time congratulating Peter on his performance. Finally, everybody in the congregation went off to lunch at some restaurant or other while I went to bed for the rest of the day. Week after week the same people came for the same service and nothing happened—except for a gradual improvement in my nervous condition. Had our white friend changed his attitude toward Blacks? Not one whit; he proclaimed his opinions loud and long. At last one of the newer and more liberal members of the church twitted him about his inconsistency. Believe it or not, the old boy had an answer. "Peter and his aunt," said he, "ain't really black!"

What had happened? Although our white friend had been faced with a challenge, that challenge had been presented in an indirect way. Neither Peter nor his aunt were threatening his living arrangements. Nobody, with the exception of myself, had been put on the spot. We were engaged in no crusade for black rights or white privileges. We were worshiping God in a small country church and enjoying one another's fellowship. The magic of the Holy Spirit worked against some very heavy odds.

Is it possible to try the Ain't-Really-Black-Method in Bypass? You are our man in town; you would know better than I. Consequently, you will have to weigh the following observations against your own knowledge.

Prejudiced people—and as far as women acolytes are concerned, I am included—are generally careful not to meet the object of their prejudgment face to face. Here, the problem is not with girls, but with girl acolytes. Could you arrange for Mrs. K. K. K. to meet some of your group of females in a natural way? Is a church school party sponsored by Mr. and Mrs. Kaltenborne a possibility? Could she become a teacher in a Bible class that included teen-aged girls? I am willing to suggest anything to her that you think she might accept, but, if you have grasped the essence of the Ain't-Really-Black-Method, I leave its precise Bypass-discharge to your imagination.

The Ain't-Really-Black-Method is only one way to tackle the task of changing prejudice, so do not let it monopolize your style. Since the great cement that holds small churches together is fellowship, let's see if it cannot be utilized in order to solve your dilemma. Despite what Mrs. K. K. K. said to me about not wanting to stir up trouble, my guess is that she has let others know about her feelings. Before too long—unless Saint Stephen's is different from any other parish I know—some of her contacts will communicate her dislike to you. That will be your opportunity to take action. Like a good Boy Scout, be prepared! Probably, the majority of your parishioners will care little one way or the other about the use of girls around the altar, but they will want to appear fair-minded and humane. Consequently, when you talk to people, stress the justice involved in using girls where heretofore only boys have been allowed. Point out that women acolytes are now found in many churches. Emphasize that women should have as many rights in the church as men (since you know my views about women's ordination, I hope you appreciate what all these statements are costing me). In talking to people, always be sympathetic to Katherine's views, but firm in your own. Then—sit back and let the rest of the congregation deal with your conservative member. Most of them will not be ready to beard her on this controversy; but church people, given time, have ways of showing their feelings without getting into elaborate arguments. I doubt if Mrs. Kaltenborne is ready to lose the friendship of the entire congregation over "female altar boys." It is even possible that in time she may come to share the majority view, which we hope will turn out to be yours. If that is too much to hope for, we can expect her to keep quiet about the matter—if you can win the rest of the congregation to your way of thinking.

Note, however, that none of this can be accomplished overnight! If denominations that have used women pastors for years still have trouble placing them, do not expect feelings about your lady acolytes to dissolve next week. Consequently, I should think that some compromise—albeit a temporary one—is now in order. Can you arrange things for the next six months so that your girls will serve at only one specific service—say the 10:00 A.M. Eucharist on Sunday? Frankly, what is wanted is a salve for Mrs. Kaltenborne. When dealing with ultraconservative people, always allow them some victory, no matter how small or inconsequential. Such a tactic allows them to keep part of their prestige; and, given human nature, that is an important consideration. Never will you win them over if you completely humiliate them.

Have you had enough of my words of wisdom? If so, to action!

If you agree, let me write to Katherine. I will acknowledge our long friendship and will state that I understand her position. Indeed, I suspect that Katherine picked me to be a patsy on this one, for my views about women's ordination

103

are well known. Then I shall do the right thing as dean and point out to our dissident lady that you are perfectly within your rights to use girls and name several parishes where this is being done. Having come to your defense, I shall pull back a bit and affirm that, since different points of view are allowed on this problem, I shall suggest to you that things be arranged so that at least one Sunday service be free from girl acolytes. In turn, this will give me the opportunity to suggest strongly to Mrs. K. K. K. that she become busy and recruit a few of her male relatives—who are currently staying away from Saint Stephen's—to receive training as altar boys. After all this, I shall go even further and tell her that I shall look forward to her membership on the new liturgical committee I am asking you to form. My thinking here is that such a body would give everybody involved a chance to express a personal opinion before such opinions get translated into confrontations. By the way, you had better chair this committee, and dealing with Katherine will take a lot of tact . . . so read the thirteenth chapter of First Corinthians before each meeting!

I have sighted the mailman. As soon as possible, let me know your reactions. And so . . .

A. M. Upchurch, Dean

# XII

# Liturgical Talk from Merry Mary

I sing of Maypoles, Hock-carts, wassails, wakes,
Of bridegrooms, brides, and of their bridal cakes.
(Herrick—*Hesperides, Argument of His Book*)

10 Church Street
Bypass, Michigan

Dear Pastor,

Am I called upon to be both the serpent and the dove? In other words, wise and naive at the same time? Probably, dear Pastor! Otherwise, I could never explain the dealings I have with the clergy—especially one Theophilus Ignatius, Principal of Jubilee Seminary and the teacher of a course known as "Practical Points in Public Worship."

Despite the ambivalence of my character, I should have known the old boy—he is ten years younger than I—had something in mind when he came to see me yesterday afternoon. I'll give him credit; he baited his hook with consummate skill. First he mentioned that his course next year was going to have several students in it from denominations other than mine. Then he extolled my vast knowledge of sixteenth- and seventeenth-century English preachers. Finally, sensing that my mood was now benign, he struck! Consequently, I have consented to deliver a lecture next year to his class on how a lay person looks at baptisms, weddings, and funerals. How does that strike you for sheer clerical cunning?

Yet, while I have a sneaking admiration for the Reverend Theophilus' gall, I have to admit he is a shrewd psychologist. He knows well enough that I have lots of ideas on the subject and that I would appreciate an opportunity to express them. For example, these rites almost always engender social gatherings in the small church, and unfortunately parsons and their flocks often differ as to the importance of these meals. Indeed, clergy and laity often have different views on lots of things connected with these ceremonies. This may generate a lot of friction in a small parish, and I would like to see an end to that. Last of all, I have the feeling that the liturgies surrounding these services might serve as a way of making the life of the small parish more dynamic—if the lay people would just take themselves more seriously.

Whew! Now that is certainly going to cover a lot of ground. Do you suppose I might get out of my depth? Since I am supremely confident, I do not suppose that I will. Still, I would appreciate it if you would look over the notes that I am making part of this letter. Then give me your opinion, but please be gentle to an old lady who wants her ideas to be relevant to the present parish situation and who hopes that she can present some creative notions. And since yours will be the only eyes to see my ramblings and since they tell me confession is good for the soul, let me express my deepest feelings and admit that I want to shake "The Reverend" up a bit. Theophilus is a dear, sharp, intellectual person—in a dull bookish sort of way—and, truth to tell, I am fed up because he finds the twentieth century so painful. The trouble, as far as Theophilus is concerned, is that these present times are still in a state of flux and the Reverend doesn't like anything that isn't bound up in leather, stamped in gold, and placed upon a library shelf. As for me—well, I like my own ideas better than those of any author. The students ought to find me quite a contrast to their principal—especially if I take Theophilus' advice and end my lecture with a rendition of "The Vicar of Bray."

And speaking of "The Vicar of Bray," you should have been with me last week when I attended my great-niece's wedding at Cranberry Portage. Things started off badly and then got worse, the climax coming when our "vicar" stepped into the pulpit, first cast his eyes upward to the roof and then back to the walls, and finally boomed, "I guess it's safe to proceed since none of the rafters and walls have collapsed at the sight of all you former church members!"

Now tell me, why do some preachers look upon weddings, funerals, and baptisms as a good chance to get in some of their favorite licks? I am certain that nobody currently staying away from that parish will be inspired to darken the doors of the church by such tactics. Why not let the liturgy and the social arrangements work to influence the congregation; and, if the parson preaches, let him limit his remarks to one positive factor in the ceremony? Perhaps you and the students at Jubilee may disagree; but, if all else fails in my lecture, allow me to make at least one point. Lay people and clergy are quite likely to see these rites from different perspectives.

Theophilus—though I dare not mention this at Jubilee— taught me that lesson many years ago when I was a mother and he was a parish pastor. At the baptism of my second daughter, every part of his body said, "Let us get this thing over with as soon as possible!" He went so fast that he reminded me of a man whose dinner was in the process of getting cold. On the other hand, it was my child who was being baptized; and this made that event important to me. I think all participating lay people will see weddings, baptisms, and funerals as memorable—especially if one of

107

their relatives or friends is involved. Therefore, my advice to the students at Jubilee—and indirectly to Theophilus—is to take these ceremonies seriously, for your lay people definitely do.

That is not the same thing as saying that strangers—or even church members—will not come to these rites with certain notions as to what they want. The intensity of these wishes seems to vary indirectly with their knowledge of church regulations—at least that is the way a former rector of Saint Stephen's used to put it. That poor man was a little jaundiced anyway—a feeling that was not helped when he was once called out of bed at dawn because of an "emergency down at the cove." The "emergency" turned out to be the nonarrival of an imported preacher, and the couple wishing to be married were afraid they would miss the effect of the dawn spreading itself over Bypass Bay!

Still, if lay people have a tendency to get too romantic over these occasions, clergy can be accused of being too regulation-conscious. Church and state rules governing these services—especially those in connection with marriage—do seem to grow yearly, don't they! Thus, I intend to suggest in my lecture that all clerics, whether in small churches or not, keep a list of the regulations governing baptism, marriages, and funerals posted in a conspicuous spot. If they wish to mail these notices, fine, but mimeographed sheets from a parish tend to end up in trash heaps. From time to time, sermons on these subjects are also appropriate—more about sermons later—but on the whole I think you will find that posted notices are the best. In this way, awkward situations may well be avoided. Nevertheless, I am not so sure that I want to avoid all awkward happenings, for a lot of them do make amusing anecdotes!

So you might say that lay people tend to see these services in a sentimental way; clergy in a realistic way. On the whole, however, and despite what some of my writing to the present might make you suppose, the laity tend to see these ceremonies in a very conservative fashion. Underlying the approach of most participants to these rites is tradition—they like to marry each other in the same way the ceremony was done for their fathers and mothers. Until a few years ago, that was entirely possible, but today there is not a Christian in America who is not aware of the liturgical changes that have affected many of the churches. Funerals, baptisms, and weddings are no exceptions. On the whole, it is your clergy and not your lay person who is interested in these modifications. In fact, "interested" is not the right term. Some people are furious at the alterations! Church congregations may love to throw rice at weddings—and not care much about the source of the custom, but wait until some older parishioner sees a closed casket in a funeral home service! He will care little for new rubrics and less for the feelings of the pastor who must work right next to a very showy corpse, but he will feel strongly that "things are not right." Custom, not discernment, affect lay thinking in these matters. With the clergy, however, things are different.

Generally, this comes about because the cleric has a professional and technical interest in the "worship" of funerals, weddings, and baptisms. And it is the newly ordained parson, fresh from seminaries like Jubilee, who is much more inclined to consider and experiment with novel ideas in these fields. It says much for these people's sense of duty to say that many of the changes now acknowledged as improvements have come about because these young clerics were willing to stick their necks out and persuade congregations to adopt new ideas. Sometimes the process has been a slow and painful one—even in those denominations described as nonliturgical—but, in my own mind at least, services are now much more meaningful. I can say this because it has often been the small parish where the battle lines were drawn. Not everybody is as pleased with this new atmosphere as Mary Walsh! But change must come because that is the way of America and the world.

Do you now know why I began this epistle by describing myself as the serpent and the dove? It is a sad fact that many a pastor, even under the old Prayer Book, chose to be neither; he preferred to keep his liturgical knowledge to himself. That was not a wise decision then or now, with the coming of so many changes . . . You and the students at Jubilee can finish that statement by yourselves!

Pastor Allen, a former rector at Saint Stephen's, used to say that the worst place to explain a funeral was at a funeral. I would extend his adage to baptisms and marriages. To some extent, it is good to allow these services to speak for themselves. Our denomination is fortunate because these rites are bound up with the rest of our services in one book, and parishioners have easy access to them—especially when sermons are dull! Despite that fact, the ignorance of the ordinary parishioner about these ceremonies is apt to be profound. A "stage" baptism or a "movie" funeral probably provides more instruction than the Prayer Book, although in the small church we are fortunate that many people still attend these rites. Nevertheless, it is no wonder that individuals will sometimes approach the clergy with strange requests when these services are to be performed.

Most Protestant denominations are in worse condition; for, when these rites are printed, one almost always finds them buried in the back of a hymnal in less than bold letters. For years I have suspected that Protestant leaders did not want their members to know about these services, despite the fact that some of them are well written and better than some parallel Anglican ceremonies. Hence, I intend to tell all the students at Jubilee, regardless of their denomination, to preach several times a year on baptisms, funerals, and weddings. Still, does that seem like too bold advice? Variations that the preacher likes could be fitted into his talk; and I am sure that most of his listeners would find such topics interesting, for it is at these ceremonies where their lives are touched most profoundly by their church.

Oh, my! I began this section of my letter by mentioning the interest of the cleric in bringing about ritual changes and ended up by arguing that the preacher should make sure that his people understand the fixed and accepted parts of these services. My only defense—it is a woman's privilege to change her mind! Yet, before getting on with the task of how change can be introduced, let me carry the notion about "fixed and accepted parts" a little further. This time it is the ignorance of some clergy that concerns me.

Once more Theophilus and my daughter's baptism comes to mind. Will the old boy never cease to serve as a bad example? At any rate, toward the end of the ceremony, Reverend Ignatius stood up and stated that there would be a party at the close of the service in the church. Party indeed! Such condescension missed the point; to me and my friends the social events surrounding baptisms, funerals, and weddings are not an extension of the rites but an integral part of them. Indeed, the feelings surrounding these gatherings are so deep that one could almost call them instinctive, or at least part of the very web and woof of the small church. Automatically, at least one woman of the parish will be assigned the task of organizing "funeral meals"; the bride and groom would not consider it a "church marriage" if there were not a reception.

It is true that in these fellowship gatherings the role of the parson becomes passive. Perhaps that is what bothered the present principal of Jubilee! In a very real way these meals can run quite well without the pastor, but still, he had better show up! It would be well if he also realized the wisdom of not outlasting his welcome—knowing how to pick up low cues has its advantages in the small parish! The truth of the matter is that no pastor can ever stand in the way of a reception's main business, which is to offer congratulations or sorrow—depending on the circumstances—over a meal. For in the small church we are a sharing partnership—a state of life that goes as far back as Jesus and his disciples. Has it ever been noticed how frequently they enjoyed food together? Seldom does the veil of history stand so thin between biblical times and the twentieth century as when a small gathering of Christians sits down to a common meal.

Given that sentiment, one might have supposed that Theophilus, with his love of the past, would have recognized not only the links of the fellowship but also the theological connections.

But that is to expect too much! Many people like Theophilus can only see the church when it is thoroughly interpreted by the past. There are lots of theologians like that, people who are afraid to take firm stands in new directions lest their statements upset a piece of their own denominational history. But why pick on theologians; parishioners in small churches like the past also. Should they be disturbed? My answer to most clerics is never—unless such a disturbance would make the fellowship of your parish even stronger.

What really bothers me is that the family intimacy, so much a part of the little parish, almost ceases when they worship together. Now, I am not oblivious to the fact that the members of a congregation sing hymns together or frequently enter into a dialogue with the officiant—he leading and they replying. But almost never is a congregation able, psychologically, to understand that they are a corporate group, seeking to unite themselves as a gathering in the work of God. Worship to a member of a small church is a one-to-one proposition. It is Jesus who "saves" the individual, but not Jesus who "saves" the group.

This attitude of individuality is really brought to the fore when we observe ourselves witnessing the rites of marriage, baptism, and burial. From liberal Protestant to conservative Catholic, the whole ritual is seen as an operation where the pastor does *something* for *somebody*. It is Reverend X who baptizes the baby, marries the couple, or buries the corpse; the church congregation sees itself as passive spectators.

When I was discussing the social aspects of our three rites, I compared the church to a family; when I discussed its worship, I stated that the analogy largely broke down. Would it not strengthen the entire concept of the small church family if everybody at worship would see the *entire* group as a functional entity?

I say yes! I also say that the small church, with its strong feeling of companionship, is well suited to put this idea of congregational worship into practice. Given the hidden structure of government in the small church, its reluctance to change, and its historical unwillingness to lead the denomination in new ideas, I admit, that does seem like a surprising statement. Paradoxically enough, I feel strongly that the rural church that survives will be the rural church that is willing to take risks. Once creativity surrenders to safe policy, the small parish will lose one of its reasons for being. Already it looks far too much to the suburbs for leadership. Indeed, the inventive forces now working at Saint Stephen's—namely, your new worship committee—has already generated a lot of heat, if not much light. Katherine has been busy spreading the word that Dean Upchurch has ordered it, and your counteragent, Joy Jones, has already dubbed it the keep-the-lid-on committee. By that she means that it is chiefly designed to make the congregation swallow the new Prayer Book. Whatever else you can say, Saint Stephen's is not dead!

And speaking of the new worship committee—

congratulations! You took me seriously when I advised you in my letter about the women's association to make sure that you consulted influential lay people before making an important move. Getting Mrs. Arthur J. Fillmore to serve on it was a work of genius. Alice, being the wife of a banker and belonging to a well-established Bypass family is a power in this parish—even though she could attend church more often. The worship committee will think twice before they disagree with her. And that includes Katherine, who admittedly is a hard case; for she has an ax to grind about the girl acolytes.

Knowing this, I would carefully keep the agenda in my own hands for a meeting or two—if I were you. Also, I would begin this committee's work with a consideration of baptisms, funerals, and weddings—do not put the Eucharist to the forefront until you succeed in having Katherine actively working for something and not spending her time raging against "female altar boys." But what could that "something" be?

Given her training and philosophy, Katherine would never agree to stand before a congregation and read—she would think that was no church job for a woman—but she might consent to sit in the congregation and lead the congregation in their prayers and responses. If you talk her into that role—Alice might help here—you will have accomplished two things. Katherine's animosity will have been turned into a positive action, and you will have converted your very passive congregation into an active, responsive one. And that—despite my feeling about its desirability—may take some doing.

At liturgical services in a small parish, most members of the congregation are very afraid of making mistakes. Therefore, the first thing your committee should do is to appoint some person who will sit in the congregation to lead them in their responses, prayers, and physical actions. If one listens to the conversations these days about the new Prayer Book, most questions are not, "What is the theological meaning of that prayer," but "When do we sit?" or "Shall we kneel or stand at this point?" A congregational leader then is a "must" appointment, and Katherine, because of her former acting experience, would be ideal. Who can tell what might grow out of this? By the time you have finished examining baptisms, funerals, and weddings, she might be ready to become an acolyte herself!

The affairs of Saint Stephen's have distracted me. Perhaps some of the students at Jubilee—especially those who come from other denominations where the emphasis is on preaching—might find my feelings about congregational participation in worship of no value. Could I then make an observation about present Protestant worship practices? Bluntly, I feel that they represent one of the worst features of medieval Catholicism!

Actually, the point is not too hard to prove. Historically— here I must bow to Theophilus—the priest was all important because it was only he who could say Mass. Indeed he did not need a congregation. At the Reformation, the Protestants threw out the Mass, but kept the priest—or at least the clerical domination of the service. Consequently, my pleas to allow congregations to have a bigger corporate share in the ceremonies of weddings, baptisms, and funerals pertains even more to liberal Protestants than it does to our denomination.

Second, it is also worth noting—for those interested in the ecumenical movement—that the standardization of the calendar governing Bible readings and the making of the Eucharist central to the service of marriage, baptism, and burial is being more readily accepted than agreements on doctrine. But that is another subject . . .

And speaking of other subjects, it is time for me to leave

this writing and concentrate on the monthly game Theophilus and I play. Each month we choose a modern subject and comment on it in Latin over the telephone. The first one who cannot translate pays for the telephone bill. The subject this month is *"Coniux, liberatem mulieris spectat"*; i.e., *"A husband looks at Women's Lib."* My first observation is, *"Nec tecum vivere possum, nec sine te."*

Now Pastor, if you want to know what that means, reply to this letter, with full remarks!

Your loving friend,
Mary Walsh

# XIII

## Is It Pleasant to Dwell in Unity? Well, Most of the Time!

Be not angry that you cannot make others as you wish them to be, since you cannot make yourself as you wish to be. (Thomas à Kempis—*Imitation of Christ*)

Canterbury Street
Palestine, Michigan

Dear Paul,

My goodness, you are upset! It is a wonder that the telephone wire between your rectory and mine did not melt last evening when you described your feelings about the Bypass Ministerial Association. Yet—a word with you please! Threatening to withdraw from this group over an unhappy experience does seem a bit drastic. There is not a clergyman alive who can say that he had always been pleased with everything his fellow pastors have done. I have no doubt that in the course of your ministry you will—probably quite innocently—upset some staid Presbyterian or Baptist pastor. To put it another way—remember that ministerial associations demand a high degree of tolerance. Believe in them, but be prepared to make allowances. Of course, as you doubtless know, there are clergy who choose to do neither. They prefer to stay away from any type of interchurch cooperation. In a very broad way, however, their congregations do not—a lesson I learned in a dramatic way many years ago.

At the time I was stationed in Cranberry Portage, which is some forty miles up the road from Bypass and is about the same type of community. When I first went there, the local parish had no hall; but eventually, after a good deal of huffing and puffing, we managed to erect a building. It turned out to be too small—What new parish hall does not? But that is another story. At any rate the time drew near for it to be dedicated, which meant a visit from the bishop. Consequently, I went to the ladies of the church just chocked full of information about the visiting dignitaries that were going to come, and requested that the women put on a reception. My message was received with glances and expressions that could only be classified as slightly below absolute zero. Finally, the president of the guild sighed, glanced at her cousin, and requested the use of the cousin's silver tray for the afternoon. The cousin squirmed but finally consented to the transaction if Madge's mother could be induced to "lend her teapot that matched it so well." This made it Madge's turn, who, after a short pause, agreed that it might be done. After another ten seconds of silence, somebody else stated that she hoped that the finger sandwiches would not have too much mayonnaise on them this time, and everybody nodded in solemn agreement. At last, being unable to stand the lowering atmosphere any longer, I opened my big mouth—innocent that I was—and volunteered that the bishop was a simple soul who would be content with store-bought cookies and coffee in paper cups. The women all listened politely and then kept right on with their elaborate schemes. Again, I made my bright remark about the self-renouncing characteristics of the bishop, adding in an even more telling voice that the other dignitaries would also be content with the simplest of fare. Once more there was a period of embarrassed silence until the secretary of the organization uncoiled her hand, gripped her walking stick with a calculated grimace, and then from her perch on an overstuffed sofa proceeded to give me a lesson in ecumenical manners that I have never forgotten. "Listen, Reverend," she began, "this organization isn't worried about the comings and goings of bishops. The gentleman in question will arrive at 3:00 P.M. and be gone by 6:00 P.M. But you," and here her voice turned deadly, "have invited several town congregations to this event. And what is more . . . we know they are coming! Now," she continued, warming to her task, "every woman in those congregations will be observing exactly how this reception runs, and despite the fact that the founder of our faith was crucified, I assure you that this guild has no intention of undergoing the same process—even if you could guarantee a resurrection on the third day! So," she concluded, banging her cane to emphasize every word, "let me give you a word of advice. You run the dedication and let us, who know how to do it, run the reception!"

Over the years I have always cherished this rather rude awakening, for it taught me some eternal truths, not only about church organizations in small towns, but also about how they view each other. One congregation will watch other churches, and in the process assess those aspects of the other denomination that interest them the most. Judging by the example I just gave you, a pastor might suppose these conclusions are always critical, but that would be a false implication. What my meeting with the ladies taught me is that a local parish always wishes to appear well in the eyes of neighboring churches. Certainly, my guild did not like being put on the spot; but, after finding themselves on one, it was determined not to be embarrassed in front of the town's other Christians. The women clearly recognized that most of the guests would not worry about the authenticity of the bishop's prayers, but the finger sandwiches . . . ah, that was another matter!

It follows then that a wise pastor always strives to put his

119

best foot forward when he is dealing with people from another congregation. When engaged in ecumenical relations concentrate on those aspects of parish life which other churches value. Always dress well for ecumenical meetings. If you are the guest preacher at another town church, make certain that your sermon is well prepared and not offensive to any theological position that parish may hold. Do your best always to be polite and courteous. And always make sure that you do not embarrass your own congregation at any of these outings! Your own flock will criticize you often enough among themselves, but do not suppose that they want other congregations to do it. Indeed, your people always hope that you will exercise clerical and social leadership in a small town. What is true of you is also true of your parish.

In this realm the sincerest form of flattery is still imitation. Frequently, exertions in one church will stir another into action. Should one church build a new rectory, expect other churches in the same town to do likewise. On this point, however, do not mistake the size of a congregation for its leadership ability; criteria here have much more to do with the respect with which a pastor and his church is held than it has to do with the numbers in its pews. Do not accuse me of saying that size is not an important factor—I am simply pointing out that there are other and more important standards for determining religious leadership in a community. A small congregation employing a long-residing clergyman and containing several old established small-town families will probably exercise as much weight as a newer church with a young pastor and three times the membership. Unfortunately, you are young as far as your length of service in Bypass is concerned; fortunately, your church does have a few well-established families. Thus, you are in a better position to exercise influence than if you were stationed in a new church.

Some clergy despise the idea of leadership in a small

town, feeling that it manipulates people or events and chokes the growth of the spirit. But please, Paul, do not disdain the role! The old biblical statement that where there is no vision the people perish is just as true for small American towns as it was for Israel. Discovering new ideas that work is, of course, not easy. Implementing them is even harder. A talented group, however, are American clergy and capable of many ideas . . . if only they will use them! Take your average ecumenical worship service as an example.

Suppose the Bypass Ministerial Association decides to hold a joint Thanksgiving service. Having met, the cooperating clergy decide—usually by a process of elimination—which parish will be the host. The pastor in charge draws up an order of worship, arranges for a choir, and prepares the sermon. On the fateful evening all the clerics with a few of their faithful in tow show up to enjoy the "ecumenical happening." Too often this service has no specific theme and less thrust. In reality it is a Presbyterian service in a Presbyterian church or a Disciples of Christ liturgy in a Disciples of Christ building. In a small town the average parishioner is not fooled by any of this. If you think he is, just check the denominational background of those present the next time you attend one of these services. In all likelihood over one half of the people present will be those who are regular attenders of that church. The membership of the other parishes will be conspicuous by its absence. Is this an ecumenical service? You can draw your own conclusions.

If we are going to improve anything, let us at least start with the practical notion that as many people as possible ought to be given a part in the service. Thus, if you are using a Nazarene church, have the Nazarenes prepare the service, find a Methodist layman to read from the Bible, use a Roman Catholic to do the preaching, persuade several Episcopalians to act as ushers, recruit the Presbyterian choir, and train a few children in the Church of God to light and

121

extinguish the candles. This will take careful planning, and everybody present will have to concede something. However, I will bet you a good steak dinner that this type of service will do more for the ecumenical movement in Bypass than a dozen guest preachers and two dozen imported choirs.

In rereading the above paragraph the expression "careful planning" caught my eye. Double the ordinary intensity of those words and raise them to the tenth power. Every action done jointly by churches in a small town needs careful planning, and ecumenical worship services are no exception. To begin, are you certain, Paul, that everybody in your local clerical union has the same meaning for the word "worship"? Frequently, people in clerical groups use the same terms, but give them different meanings. Again, is everybody certain as to the aims of their union exercises? In what way are they superior or inferior to what people do in their own parishes week after week? One reason why the ecumenical movement does not proceed beyond the first stage in small towns is because these types of questions are seldom asked, for parishes prefer to do things out of habit rather than out of a conviction that has been fostered by earnest face-to-face investigation.

To return briefly to the reason this letter is being written. You have been confronted, as indeed all small-town clergy are, with a local ministerial association; and you have weighed it in the balance and been disappointed in at least one of its actions. Rest assured that many in your community do not share your feelings.

Communities expect these type of clergy groupings to exist and for some very sound reasons. Frequently, ministerial unions can do emergency social service work or serve as the cutting edge in community education. Again, clerical organizations give a sense of harmony where disunity is obvious. Nobody—omitting depth psychologists, of course—likes disharmony. If this sounds too much like a statement from a public relations man, consider the one great thing a ministerial association did for me many years ago in a small New Mexican town. In this community all the children met in the basement of the Episcopal parish—it happened to be the largest—but every clergyman in that organization contributed something to it. It is/was my fortune to have for a number of years an elderly, earnest Disciples of Christ preacher as a Bible teacher. The passage of thirty years has scarcely dimmed the power of the lessons taught by this earnest man, dressed in his Sears-Roebuck best. Thanks to him, when I entered seminary I had a knowledge of the subject that enabled me to win prizes consistently in Scripture. Had not the clergy in that New Mexican town seen a need and cooperated to solve the problem, the foundations of my professional biblical knowledge could not have been laid.

Do not suppose that I spend all my time singing the praises of interchurch cooperation. Weaknesses are too obvious. Clergy groups, like every other organization, like to plan things so they can obtain the quickest result at the lowest cost. Things such as joint worship services, UNICEF drives, and CROP rallies appeal because most members will agree that these operations serve a need, are highly visible, and speedily finished. Long-term goals, however, are quite another matter.

Ministerial groups seldom see themselves as part of the universal church which stretches back through the ages; their aims are much more likely to be immediate. Consequently, they seldom try to improve local preaching or pastoral abilities. Study as such is generally considered a personal matter; and, although many small-town pastors do it, they seldom share their newfound knowledge with each other. Again, small town clergy seldom act as one another's assessors on such things as Bible classes or worship services. So—break some precedents and do it in

Bypass! And finally, do not forget the excellent role that ministerial associations can play in aiding clergy.

Let me introduce this final idea by reciting an old cliche—the one that runs "Where does the pastor go when the pastor needs a pastor?" "To the bishop," you reply, but bishops are busy men and probably cannot spare you the time these pastoral situations take. How much does the bishop know about Bypass anyway? Paul! Your best advisors are not at diocesan headquarters, but right in your own hometown. Many clergymen—especially liberal Protestants—are very good at counseling and even better at understanding the wants, the dreams, and sins of their contemporaries. Everybody needs a "soul friend"—as the ancient Irish used to say—and members of clerical groups can perform this function in quite relaxed ways. Have you ever noticed how many parsons use ministerial associations as sounding boards for their own frustrations, triumphs, and problems? Here is a place to describe difficulties with choirs and successes with young people. It is quite true that listeners can seldom do much in hard cases—except to listen, extend sympathy, and keep quiet; but even these acts can be of great worth. Fault-finding associations are as numerous as the grains of sand on most of the ocean beaches of the world; helping groups are much more rare. If you ever discover one, Paul, cultivate it carefully, for it is a pearl of great price.

Enough! Writer's cramp has long ago entered into my wrist and is extending up my arm. Let another Paul sum up this letter:

"He who plants and he who waters are equal and each shall receive his wages according to his labor. For we are all fellow workmen for God."

A. M. Upchurch, Dean

# Epilogue

## Bringing Up Father

There is a measure in all things. (Horace)

Saint Stephen's Church
Bypass, Michigan

Dear Bishop Cranmer,

If C. S. Lewis could speak of the pilgrim's regress, I hope you will not mind if I discuss a parson's advance. Let this "advance" be in both physical and spiritual terms, and let the physical lead into the spiritual . . .

After my prayers and housework were done this morning, I decided to be like Buddha and sit under a meditation tree. My spot for this sort of thing is located under an old gnarled maple tree that has stood for nearly a hundred years on Matching Mountain—that tall hill that overlooks both Bypass and the inland sea called Huron. From this spot, I can always make out the steeple of Saint Stephen's, for its white cross set against the dark blue of the lake dominates the town. The cold spring wind made me move every now and then, and every time I did a piece of paper crackled in my hip pocket. No need to read it; yesterday I memorized its contents. ". . . should you come as my assistant to Country Club Hills, this will be a wonderful opportunity to learn. Now you will be close to the mainstream of this diocese and the church. Think how well it will equip your future ministry."

I thank neither God nor the new rector of Grace Church,

Country Club Hills, for placing temptation in my way. He is quite right; Grace Church is in the mainstream of this present age's thinking, but Saint Stephen's Bypass is not. Should I accept the invitation, I shall be far more attractive to a search committee looking for a rector; if I stay at my present post for twenty years, most of the residents of this diocese won't even know who I am, let alone where I live.

This denomination moves by pressure groups, and most pressure groups are not interested in the small parish. It is the questions of the moment that they see—the building for the future or the vision of the past is of small import. Sometimes I wonder what Herbert, Herrick, Wesley, and Barth—those small-town people who contributed to seventeenth-century English poetry, left an evangelical movement that is mighty yet, and brought forth a theology that dominates reformed Christianity—would have been like had they seen the church as modern America so often does. Would they have dominated Country Club Hills, or would Country Club Hills have dominated them?

At the present moment American Christians like their religion the same way they like their breakfast cereal—instantly. I may be pardoned if I disagree. Well does Saint Paul compare it to a battle, the Epistle to the Hebrews compare it to a race, and John Bunyan compare it to a pilgrimage. It is a question, you see, of growing into "the measure of the stature of the fullness of Christ."

Certainly "the church" gives us plenty of opportunity to grow. I am always going to training sessions for clergy—a pleasant diversion from the essence of my job. I am especially fond of those symposiums that use the "model technique." There is the "psychiatric model" where I become a junior psychologist; the "revolutionary model" that tells me about the evils done to women and minorities throughout the world; the "social work model" that wants me to become an agent for change in society. They are all interesting, but none has so far helped me into "the measure of the stature of the fullness of Christ." And none of them has challenged me like Saint Stephen's, for it is here that I have been forced to come face to face with myself.

"Know thyself," said the Delphic Oracle. In the small church there is not much between you and your personal capacity, for financial resources are limited and so are people. You yourself learn to cope—or you become unhappy; you yourself learn to swallow your ego—or you become an emotional case; you yourself learn how to pray—for that has to become your main resource.

So, you see, I am not afraid that I could not do the work that will be demanded of me at Grace Church, Country Club Hills; but I am afraid that the lessons learned with so much pain at Bypass have not yet settled into my soul. Give me a little more time; let the small church continue to train me to rely on God and not on programs, work, and my own nerve. In time I feel certain that I shall have advanced enough to know true Christian values from those that appear to be true—but that time is not yet.

To a busy executive like yourself, this may be hard to understand—especially since your parochial ministry was spent in the suburbs. I have no intention, I assure you, of staying in Bypass forever; that would be unfair to the parish and unfair to myself. However, I trust that when I do leave, Bypass will have found my ministry as rich for itself as I have found it for myself.

By 3:00 P.M. today, my meditation had reached that stage outlined above, and for the moment I could see no reason to go further. The wind was getting colder; it was time to go home. Slowly, I withdrew the letter from my pocket, tore it up, and watched it blow across the mountain . . .

With all good wishes,
The Reverend Paul Stanbury, Pastor
Saint Stephen's Church
Bypass, Michigan

The Small Town Church

Suggestions for Further Reading

*General*

Carroll, Jackson W., ed. *Small Churches Are Beautiful*. New York: Harper & Row, 1977. Some excellent essays on the small church. Others need to be read critically.

Dudley, Carl S. *Making the Small Church Effective*. Nashville: Abingdon, 1978. Probably the best book yet written on the small church. Important also for its bibliography.

Schaller, Lyle. *Hey, That's Our Church*. Nashville: Abingdon, 1975. This prolific author has a vast knowledge of the small church.


*Personal Pastoral Challenges*

Beck, Aaron T., consultant. *The History of Depression*. New York: Psychiatric Annals, 501 Madison Ave., 1977. Although written for medical people, this is a valuable and readable study.

Chafetz, Dr. Morris. *Why Drinking Can Be Good for You*. Briarcliff Manor, N.Y.: Stein & Day, 1976. Many will find the work controversial, but I feel this psychiatrist makes some points.

James, William. *Varieties of Religious Experience*. New York: Doubleday, 1978. A classic. Read lectures IV through VIII and compare them to my approach to the "once born" and the "depressed cleric."

Kirk, Kenneth E. *Some Principles of Moral Theology*. New York: Longmans Green, 1948. Despite its age, the reader will find it enlightening to contrast Kirk's approach to the soul with modern ethical theories and much in modern psychotherapy.

128